Rosa rubiginosa "Janett's Pride"

English Rose "Shropshire Lass"

Art nouveau arbor, ornately framed by charming, small-flowered climbing roses. "Minnehaha" left and "Excelsa" right. Scene in the Deutschen Rosarium VDR, Westfalenpark in Dortmund, Germany.

Otto Bünemann
Jürgen Becker

ROSES

The most beautiful roses for large and small gardens

Design ideas for rose arbors, trellises, and beds

Rose Know-how: Planting, culture, pruning, overwintering

Consulting Editor: Dennis W. Stevenson
Administrator, Harding Laboratory
The New York Botanical Garden

Color photographs by Jürgen Becker

Drawings by György Jankovics

BARRON'S

Contents

Rose KNOW-HOW
Getting to Know Roses, Culture, Propagation

Cupid among the climbing roses

This rose has gone around the world—"Gloria Dei"

A cozy corner with "Apothecary Rose," *Rosa gallica* "Officinalis"

Hybrid Tea "Papa Meilland"

Standard roses enhance small gardens too

Fragrant potpourri of roses in a basket

Rosy Times for Your Garden

A Word First

The market for roses is changing. Roses are no longer merely mass market products. People want not only those all-of-a-kind rose beds but also fragrant rose arbors, rose-bedecked house walls, and roses in borders with garden flowers. No doubt about it: The rose has regained her primary place in the garden—her role as "queen of the flowers" has been rediscovered!

Along with this change comes a new way of handling roses. More and more gardeners want a nontoxic garden and are making an effort to use biological methods, avoiding reliance on chemical fertilizers and pesticides. This objective is more easily accomplished with healthy, naturally resistant varieties.

It's time for a contemporary rose book. This one opens a new chapter on roses.

Rose Know-how

Clear, easily read, and easy to remember, these sections present the collected horticultural know-how for roses—beginning with culture throughout the year and continuing with pruning and overwintering, disease prevention, and biological pest control. In addition, you will learn how to propagate roses, make grafts, or even breed them yourself. You'll become an expert in matters of rose culture and breeding.

Designing with Roses

Roses are wonderfully easy to combine with shrubs, grasses, perennials, or annual garden flowers. But they can do even more: As climbers on trees, arbors, espaliers, and pergolas, forming garlands, or as bedding or shrub roses, they create an aesthetically charming neighborhood. Examples of design in brilliant color photographs will produce ideas and give you the urge to try them out.

Rose Portraits

There are over 300 of the most beautiful as well as the hardiest rose species to choose from: old roses, English roses, wild roses, climbing roses, and robust ground-covering roses, among which also there are many repeat-blooming and fragrant varieties. Here you will also find the world stars among the hybrid teas and the lushly blooming floribunda roses.

In addition, on the book flaps you are introduced to two of the most newly popular groups of roses: roses of the olden days (old roses) and natural beauties (wild roses).

The authors and editors wish you lots of fun and good luck with your roses.

Author

Dr. Otto Bünemann, internationally respected rose expert, has been director of the German Rosarium VDR in Westfalenpark and of the Botanical Garden Rombergpark, Dortmund, since 1975. He also directs the Dortmund rose seminars. Furthermore, he is initiator of the School Biology Center in Dortmund.

Photographer

Jürgen Becker studied painting and film and for the last 12 years has been a freelance photographer for well-known book and calendar publishers as well as for international newspapers and magazines. He specializes in photographing gardens, plants, architecture, and landscapes.

Acknowledgments

The author is grateful to Mandred Klose, the head gardener in the German Rosarium until 1986, as well as to Katrin Uter, Director of the Rose Fanciers Club Hannover, for their review of the manuscript; also to Susanne Kerber of the Department for Plant Protection of Münster, district office Unna, for advice about plant protection, to Professor Georg Timmermann for looking over the text on central European wild roses, and to Ewald Scholle of Seppenrade for advice on breeding and propagation of roses. Special thanks are owed to Ewald Scholle's wife Karin for her support, as well as for making the tables and for putting the manuscript into the computer. The author also thanks his creative, all-seeing, tactful editors, Gisela Keil and Anita Kellner, of the GU Nature Books staff.

The photographer is grateful to his wife, Doris Schlaback-Becker, for her support and assistance on this book.

Important: To ensure that your pleasure in roses is not spoiled, please read the Important Notice on page 159.

Coupe d'Hébé is a marvelously fragrant Bourbon rose that blooms only once. It grows 6 feet (2 m) tall.

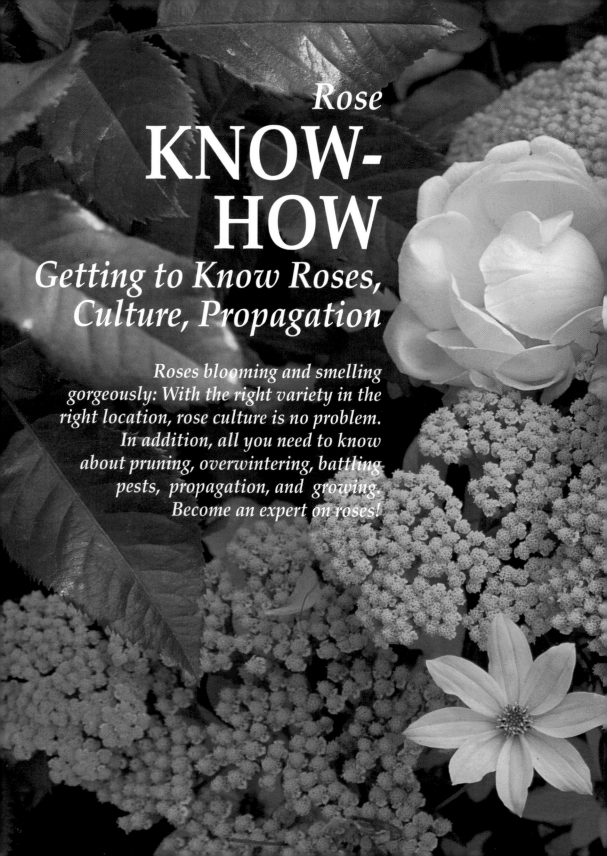

Rose

KNOW-HOW

*Getting to Know Roses,
Culture, Propagation*

*Roses blooming and smelling
gorgeously: With the right variety in the
right location, rose culture is no problem.
In addition, all you need to know
about pruning, overwintering, battling
pests, propagation, and growing.
Become an expert on roses!*

Resembling a heavily
embroidered Gobelin tapestry,
a tone-on-tone composition
of yellow shrub roses, yarrow
(Achillea millefolium hybrid),
and coreopsis

9

The Diversity of
ROSES

*The ancestors of all rose hybrids are the wild roses. A beautiful example is **Rosa pendulina**, the alpine hedge rose (see photograph above). Its dark-rose-colored flowers can still be seen in the Alps today. Wild roses have developed their simple beauty and unpretentiousness freely in nature without human interference. This distinguishes them from the cultivated hybridized rose.*

F or over 2500 years the rose has been known as the "Queen of the Flowers." Over the millennia this very symbolic flower has accompanied human beings, delighted them, and reassured them again and again.

The Arabians understood the art of obtaining rose water and attar of roses. The Romans valued the rose as the expression of the highest standard of living. And with her famous palace rose garden, the Empress Josephine in the nineteenth century made the rose popular all over Europe.

The Name of the Rose

Who when hearing the word "rose" thinks immediately of the simple wild rose with its five petals? And yet this very simple flower form is the ancestor of the rose and of the entire rose family. From this "rosette" nature has allowed the development in various locations of an unbelievable multiplicity of colors, forms, and plant shapes.

To bring the abundance of plants into a clearly surveyable form, the great Swedish botanist Carl Linnaeus (1707–1778) set up a classification system using Latin names.

Our native dog rose, for instance, is botanically classified as follows:

<u>Plant family:</u> The dog rose, like all roses, belongs to the woody plants and thus to the rose family (Rosaceae), along with the apple, plum, cherry, and apricot.

<u>Genus name:</u> The Latin name *Rosa* indicates the genus.

<u>Species name:</u> Added to the genus name is a second word that indicates the species—in the case of the dog rose, *Rosa*

"Raubritter" is one of the most frost-hardy rambler roses and therefore is recommended as a cascade, hanging, or weeping rose, despite some mildew.

The Diversity of ROSES

canina. Latin genus and species names are internationally uniform and are always written in italics. Crosses of two species are designated with an "*x,*" as, for example, *Rosa x kordesii.*

Name of the describer: To avoid confusion, the name of the describer of a species—usually abbreviated—is given after the species name. The dog rose was described by Linnaeus himself and thus it is written *Rosa canina* L.

Variety name: On the other hand, the many rose crosses, the so-called varieties, are given invented names by the particular breeders and these are indicated by quotation marks—for example, the world-famous "Gloria Dei."

If a variety has descended directly from one of the wild roses, the original species will sometimes be indicated, for example, *Rosa canina* "Kiese."

Categories of Roses

The fullness of rose flowers (termed *double*ness), their family characteristics, and their possible uses require still another arrangement from the botanical one.

Wild Roses

Wild roses (see Rose Portraits, pages 86–93) are the rose species that occurred in nature.

Their natural habitat is the northern hemisphere of the earth, that is, the temperate climate regions. Wild roses have not allowed themselves to become adjusted to tropical heat and to settle in the southern hemisphere—except with human help.

The form of the wild rose varies. These roses can cover the ground like a carpet, form shrubs or bushes, and even climb. Of course not every single-flowered rose is a wild rose. It might be a rose that has been bred to have wild rose characteristics.

Hybrid Roses

Most of these, which have come from crossbreeding of the original roses, are categorized according to their use as bedding roses, shrub roses, climbing roses, and dwarf or miniature roses. In addition, there are the ground-cover roses, cascade roses, and standards (tree roses) as distinct "use groups," which partially overlap with the conventional groups.

Climbing roses (see Rose Portraits, pages 94–103): These are classified according to flowering or growth habit.

• Blooming habit: Many varieties bloom only once and therefore are very similar to the wild climbing roses. Next there are a whole string of repeat-blooming varieties that after the first flowering in June—often with a brief interval—will put forth again and bloom continuously until fall.

• Growth habit: A distinction is made between climbing roses with erect, stiff canes (climber) and those with soft, flexible canes (rambler).

Shrub roses (see Rose Portraits, pages 104–123): They are classified as once-flowering and repeat-flowering.

Ground-covering roses (see Rose Portraits, pages 124–131): These are grouped according to low-growing or higher-growing varieties. They are classified into four growing types all told (see page 124). Thus, the section on ground-covering roses includes not only the low-growing, creeping climbing roses but also broad or weeping shrub roses as well as densely branching cluster-flowered bedding roses.

Bedding roses (see Rose Portraits, pages 132–149): Because all bedding roses have been repeat-flowering since their origin, different characteristics for distinction are needed here: the size of the flower and the inflorescence.

• The large-flowered roses are, in general, identical to the hybrid teas, the "true roses." Their flowers are large, usually occur one to a stem, and in every instance are double. Many varieties are fragrant.

• The cluster-flowered ones are double, semidouble, or single and always grow several to one stem in umbels or panicles.

Dwarf or miniature roses: These roses are not classified any further. They are all low-growing and continuously flowering. Whether a variety is more individual-flowering or more cluster-flowering is of no importance in view of the small size of the flowers.

The Development of Modern Garden Roses

Wild roses must have interested people in various regions for perhaps more than five thousand years. But today we can no longer recon-

Climbing roses like "Bobbie James" (back) and "New Dawn" (right) wind around a pergola. In front bloom lady's-mantle (yellow green) and cranesbill (pink).

struct their pathway to domestication.

In the Europe of the Middle Ages numerous roses were already recognized and were cultivated principally as holy plants or food plants in monastery gardens.

The Old Roses
Until the eighteenth century in Europe there were, except for wild roses, mainly different varieties of Gallica, Damask, Alba, and Centifolia roses, which all—except for Damask roses—bloomed only once. Fragrance is common to many old roses. When roses came from China around 1750, crosses with them produced new groups of roses that consistently bloomed more often:

• Portland roses (with stronger colors than most Damask roses),

• Bourbon roses (already definitely repeat-flowering),

• Noisette roses (usually cluster-flowering, but quite large flowers and good repeat-flowering),

The Diversity of ROSES

• Tea roses (very doubled flowers, but a variety that is rarely winter-hardy in cold climates),

• Hybrid perpetual roses (large flowers, strong colors, stiff stems, prominent thorns, and markedly more frost-hardy than tea roses). These can be regarded as the link between old and modern roses.

Large-flowered Roses

Probably the best-known modern garden roses are the hybrid teas. Through the influence of their Chinese inheritance from the tea rose they are repeat-blooming from the main flowering in June until the first hard frost, but they are less frost-hardy than the once-blooming roses. Today we use the term "hybrid tea" to mean only those large-flowered bedding roses whose flowers, as a rule, are born one to a stem.

The Chinese roses introduced new colors, especially a strong red, to the hybrid teas. However, many of these crosses have inherited the susceptibility to rust and spot anthracnose from their ancestors. The first breakthrough to healthy hybrid teas was achieved in 1945 by grower Francis Meilland with his

yellow hybrid tea "Gloria Dei" (see also page 132).

Cluster-flowered Roses

Besides the "large-flowered roses" there are the so-called polyanthas. They flower in clusters—that is, panicles, umbels, or just bunches. Today we include them and the floribundas, which came from them, in the cluster-flowered category.

Polyantha roses are mostly repeat-blooming or even ever-blooming varieties. What was more obvious than to cross the hybrid tea with the polyantha rose to create something new?

The barbed-wire rose, *Rosa sericea pteracantha*, bears bloodred prickles along with fine bristles.

The variety "Gruss an Aachen," from the grower Geduldig (1908), was the first floribunda rose. The development was promoted by the Danish grower Svend Poulsen, who wanted to develop a rose that would bloom as lushly as possible in the short Scandinavian summer and would nevertheless be frost-hardy.

Miniature roses, dwarf bengal roses, dwarf roses: These three terms are used as synonyms for very low-growing—scarcely taller than 12 in. (30 cm)—repeat-blooming roses whose canes are thin and have short spaces between leaves (internodes). These are the only garden roses whose leaves often have only three leaflets. They have been very successful marketed as container roses. In the garden they remain only moderately popular because they are prone to disease.

Climbing Roses

Wild roses that creep over the ground like *Rosa wichuraiana* Crép. and those that grow up into trees and shrubs like *Rosa multiflora Thunb.* are the natural originating forms for climbing roses.

From *Rosa multiflora* (see photo, page 91) the variety "Carnea" was introduced in England as early as

1804. Since almost all the varieties that have come from "Carnea," like it, bloom only once, they later regrettably lost their importance. Now extant are only "Veilchenblau" (1909; see photo, page 98), "Maria Lisa" (1925; see photo, page 99), and "Chevy Chase" (1939; see photo, page 153).

Rosa wichuraiana (see photo, page 91) arrived in Germany from Japan in 1861. But only after 1900 did the numerous crossings with it and the closly related *Rosa luciae* become famous, like "American Pillar" (1905; see photo, page 98) and the world-fa-

The grace of the wild rose is still apparent in this Lambertiana rose "Arndt" (1913), a repeat-blooming climbing rose that has value as a rarity (above). *Rosa rugosa* and its varieties possess striking hips (right).

mous "New Dawn" (1930; see photo, page 97).

Rosa x kordesii only appeared in 1940, when grower Wilhelm Kordes sowed one of the rare hips of the almost sterile hybrid species "Max Graf." But it was never successful commercially. It became famous only as a parent species for countless repeat-blooming climbing and shrub roses, although it blooms only once itself.

The Modern Crosses

Here the boundaries between the groups grow increasingly blurred because new combinations of hitherto separate qualities and characteristics appear especially attractive. Today the goals are fragrance and robustness.

15

Rose **KNOW-HOW:** *Botany*

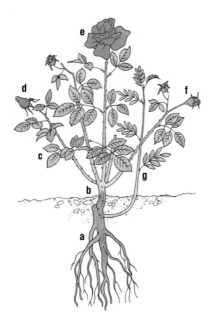

1 <u>Structure of a rose</u>
a Root
b Bud union
c Leaf
d Bud
e Flower
f Hip (fruit)
g Wild cane

The rose, botanical name *Rosa,* is a woody plant and belongs to the family of Rosaceae. Among its relatives are such varied plants as the apple tree and cherry, strawberry and hawthorn, goatsbeard and lady's-mantle. All rose varieties, which have been calculated to number more than 20,000, stem directly or indirectly from wild roses.

Like most plants, a rose consists of the root in the earth and the stem above the ground.

Root (see drawing 1a)
The rose root grows especially deep in the ground. This not only provides a good anchor but also promotes the best possible water supply even in long periods of drought. By means of cell generation and the stretching growth of the cells, the root tips drive into the earth like a nail into wood. Behind the growing zone of the young cells the root hairs grow from the cells of the outer skin (epidermis). They take in water and the nutrients dissolved in it.

Bud Union
(see drawing 1b)
The bud union is the joint between the root and the stem. For roses the union is very important, for this is where the graft is made, except in the case of tree roses (see KNOW-HOW: Propagating and Grafting, pages 58–59).

Shoot
In the rose, the shoot consists of the base cane or a stem, the young year-old canes (or branches), as well as the leaves, the buds, and the flowers or later fruits, which are called hips.

Leaves (see drawing 1c)
The leaves are always alternate and consist of 3, but often 5, 7, 9, or even up to 15 oval or elliptical, toothed leaflets. The surface of the leaves can be smooth or hairy on one side or both sides. Rose leaves vary from delicate and thin to leathery-tough, from dull to glossy, from brownish red when new to all shades of green.

Buds (Eyes)
The buds are formed in the leaf axils and in roses are often called "eyes." They frequently have on their sides "sleeping" (that is, dor-

mant) "side eyes," recognizable as tiny red points. Normally these do not sprout unless they are stimulated to do so, for instance by cutting away the large part of the stem directly over the eye (see KNOW-HOW: Propagating and Grafting, pages 58–59).

Prickles
The prickles (often called spines) sit directly on the cortex. Different from thorns and true spines, they can be rubbed away without seriously injuring the cortex. The expression "no rose without thorns" is also incorrect from the botanical point of view. The form of prickle varies from needlelike bristles to

2 Single flower

5 Cup-shaped flower

hook-shaped, extremely broad-winged, or triangular ones. Prickles can serve the rose, a so-called "spreading climber," for climbing. They scarcely keep wild animals from chewing on them at all. In just a few rose species there are also prickleless forms, for example, *Rosa pendulina, Rosa banksiae,* and *Rosa multiflora.*

Flowers (see drawing 8)
The flowers may be situated alone on a short stem or longer stem or in clusters. Swelling from the stem, the gynoecium is enclosed in a floral cup (inferior) in which are found the carpels, each with an ovary and a stigma. Around the carpels, arranged like a wreath, are the stamens, which produce the pollen.

When the pollen is dusted onto a stigma, it sprouts like a seed and forms a pollen tube, which grows through the ovary to the ovule inside. There it fertilizes an egg cell with its contents by karyogamy. The seeds develop from the egg cells. If none of the egg cells is fertilized, the ovary falls off.

Inflorescence: The flowers can occur singly or in bunches of several on large, many-flowered clusters or rather flat or spherical clustered racemes. These usually bear stunted foliage or no foliage at all.

The number of petals amounts to 5 for every one of the wild roses in the world. The single exception is *Rosa sericea* Lindl. from the Himalayas. This usually has 4 petals

8 **Structure of a flower**
a **Ovary**
b **Carpels**
c **Sepals**
d **Petals**
e **Stamens, between them the
   stigma on the pistil**

and only occasionally 5. With the hybrid teas the number varies from the single flowers (see drawing 2), which have fewer than 8 petals, to the semidouble (see drawing 3) with 8 to 20 petals, to the very double with as many as 70 or more petals.
    The form of the flowers depends on the number and form of the petals. There are urn-shaped ones (see drawing 6), rounded, cup-shaped ones (see drawing 5), rosette-shaped ones (see drawing 4), quartered ones (see drawing 7), star- and carnation-shaped ones as well as shapeless floppy flowers.

3 **Loosely doubled flower**

4 **Rosette-shaped flower**

6 **Urn-shaped flower**

7 **Quartered flower**

The Right Location for
ROSES

Roses are sun worshippers and love a gentle breeze. Even flower color and scent are dependent on sun, soil, and temperature. In optimal locations "Frühlingsduft" develops huge bushes and blooms luxuriantly in May. Often it again gives cause for delight in August with a modest repeat-flowering.

The native wild roses have been adapting well to North American conditions for thousands of years, which cannot always be said of our hybridized cultivated roses. Through crosses with species that have come from other climates, the newly developed varieties have also inherited a preference for their original climate. Therefore, the placement of the plant in the garden also plays an important role in its well-being. "Sun traps," "cold lakes," and soggy ground are not appreciated at all.

What Roses Love

Ecology—a word used to mean many things—translated from the Greek literally means "knowledge of home." Applied to plants it means nothing else but knowledge of location. For their part, climate, soil, and position again consist of many factors that influence each other and have an effect on the plant. If you know about them, you can offer your roses the kind of life that suits them.

Soil Requirements

• The soil should be deeply cultivated, porous, rich in nutrients, crumbly, and well aerated, because the roots of roses also need oxygen.

• It should drain off excess water quickly but nevertheless should have good water-retention capabilities so as not to dry out too rapidly.

The pH value should be between 6.2 and 7.1. Roses thrive best in a slightly acid, neutral to weakly alkaline soil.

A well-tilled loamy soil fulfills this requirement in fact. It is the ideal soil for roses and is usually characterized by lots of humus, loose, crumbly structure, and intense activity of soil organisms.

Sandy ground can be made more retentive and organic with the regular addition of humus.

Hard, compacted soils are not appreciated by roses.

Often, however, even soggy soil can be considerably improved with a drainage system.

Soggy soils are not suitable for roses. You can tell soggy soil by its black color and the often smeary organic structure. It's possible to change soggy, acid soil with too low a pH to one with a pH that roses will tolerate, by the

The rose arbor with "New Dawn" forms the framework for an inviting garden scene. The focal point is the stone vase in the foreground with various hens and chicks and houseleek species of the genera *Sedum* and *Sempervivum*.

careful addition of lime over several years.

The "finger test" lets you find out what kind of soil you have. Take a tablespoon of damp earth in your hand.

• With primarily sandy soil you'll feel the single grains of sand rough between your fingers. The earth will neither stay in your hand nor allow you to shape it.

Enchanted garden with surprises. The small shrub rose "Eye Opener" in the foreground combines with delphinium and other perennials. "Veilchenblau" (right) grows rampant over the pergola, while glowing from the background "New Dawn" transforms the old country house into a Sleeping Beauty's castle.

• Loamy soil feels velvety-floury and allows itself to be shaped and caught in the fingers.

• Clay soil can be shaped like dough. It feels greasy and if you run your fingers along the soil sample, it leaves a shiny surface.

Except for clay and soggy soils, all soil types are acceptable to roses.

Extremes of Climate Undesirable

Roses tolerate our climate but they suffer during extremes or continuously stressful conditions.

Extreme cold:

• Only the once-blooming roses accomplish their new growth in the summer, allowing it to mature until fall, and by the onset of winter they are in a dormant phase in which frost cannot injure them.

• Repeat-blooming roses, on the other hand, possess genes from the China roses, which are native to regions with milder winter climates and do not have a dormant period. A hybrid tea will form new shoots with flowers in winter temperatures between 59°F (15°C) and 77°F (25°C). It reacts to colder temperatures only with an obvious reduction of growth. But the green wood can easily be injured by frost.

Thus as a rule the once-blooming roses are hardier than the repeat-bloomers. Thanks to crossing and selection, repeat-blooming roses that are somewhat frost-hardy despite their China rose inheritance have been developed.

Important: Hollows, into which cold air flows during frost and pools, like a lake, are not suitable locations for tender garden roses. In such spots, late autumn frosts can repeatedly destroy new growth or even the first flowers. Extremes of winter cold can occur there.

On the other hand, inclines capitalize on the down-flow of cold air, but in southern exposures, this can lead to tissue injury through the action of frost and sun as well as to scalding the flowers in high summer and desiccation of the plants and flowers.

Drought and lack of wind lead to insect infestation. The rose suffers from spider mites and aphids or blackspot more than from "real" drying out of leaves and branches. The deep-reaching roots of the rose usually provide the plant with sufficient water even during prolonged drought. Therefore, well-rooted roses need additional water only in exceptional circumstances. When watering, it's better to thoroughly water once than to merely wet the surface more often.

Wind: Extreme heat and extreme cold are both intensified in effect by wind. Light wind is desirable, as we've said; drafts and strong winds, on the other hand, less so. There should be no chance of heat pools developing at windless times, since these promote disease and pests (see above).

Varieties that are susceptible to mildew are better when cool breezes can blow through them. Varieties at risk for spot anthracnose should be placed in fast-drying, open places in full sun.

Precipitation: Whether you live in a region with much or little rainfall is not crucial for roses if they have well-prepared, well-drained soil. Also, frequent storms needn't keep the gardener from having roses. A light wind quickly dries off the excess water.

Unpropitious, however, are extremely humid and foggy conditions, for the high humidity promotes the attack of fungus diseases such as blackspot. Often the protection of a house wall is enough to make such conditions possible for roses.

The climbing rose decorates the spot: Country idyll created with "Fugue," a hybrid from Meilland in 1958.

The Right Location for ROSES

Sun and Light

Roses are quite light- and sun-thirsty, so you should always offer them a full-sun location in the garden. Certainly there are some rose species and varieties that will also thrive sufficiently well in light semi-shade (see Rose Portraits, page 82–153). Pooled heat is to be avoided.

Careful of winter sun: What is good in summer doesn't necessarily go for winter. Within a very few hours great tensions may occur in the tissues between the sunny and the shady side of a succulent rose cane. The cane may rupture inside and then die back.

A further danger is drying. When the ground is frozen the rose roots can't take up water. Nevertheless, stored water is evaporated through the canes, so that a water deficit arises. There are several possibilities, from hilling to covering with pine boughs or burlap, to help the rose minimize its evaporation and to avoid tissue strains (see KNOW-HOW: Overwintering, pages 38–39).

The Soil Lives

The further a soil deviates from the described ideal soil, the more important are the humus content and the cultivation of soil life through additions of rotted organic materials. Countless microorganisms and multitudes of different soil-dwelling animals, from worms to crustacea to insects and even small mammals, work around the clock in such soil, churning it and thus opening it up for the plant roots.

Our Earthworm Coworkers

The earthworm is the most important organism for the soil structure. It eats dead plant parts—for example, old leaves or stable dung—and in so doing also removes the mineral soil components. Then in its digestive tract it mixes the organic substances with the clay minerals of the soil and excretes them as a fine humus. The worm's digestion produces the so-called clay-humus complexes, which provide for the desirable friability of the soil. This is more important to make roses thrive than giving them the perfect nutrients, and it eases the roots' access to the soil particles and soil capillaries.

However, the earthworms not only are humus producers but also provide for the mechanical tilling of the soil by their passage through it. This action results in good aeration and water access. Many other animals do similar work in the soil. Even the mole, which lives on many of these soil animals, brings about soil improvement with its digging. The soil organisms are thus the best coworkers for the gardener.

What Is Soil Exhaustion?

When poor growth occurs from the replanting of the same plant species in the same ground, people talk of "soil exhaustion." This happens only with some plant species or families. With the rose family it is especially common—also, for example with fruit trees.

When does soil exhaustion appear? It only occurs when roses have been planted in a soil where roses have been before. So a rose can display robust, healthy growth without any disturbance for decades in one and the same spot, while moderately close by a newly planted rose may inexplicably be failing. Such soil exhaustion seems to occur more severely and more dangerously in light, sandy soils than in loam with a high portion of clay minerals.

The toxin hypothesis: It has been proposed that the metabolite excretions from the rose roots—for example, species-specific poisons (toxins)—remain in the ground when these roses are removed. Presumably the materials later inhibit the growth of the newly planted rose roots. Normally an established plant opens up new soil areas because its root network continually grows outward, and thus never grows into its own old root channels.

With a new planting, the growth pattern may be different. The roots remaining in the soil from the uprooted plant decompose and thus form fine channels of humus in the soil. The young roots of the newly set plant gladly grow along these channels, possibly because of diminished resistance, but there they come into contact with the poisons (toxins) in or along the edges of these channels, with the result that their development is inhibited.

This concept has by no means been scientifically proven; however, it does fit with my own experience.

Perfection draws the eye to the single flower. *Rosa centifolia variegata* "Village Maid" shows a slight mottling in the bud, which later blends in.

Experience from Practice
Tests conducted over four years with the varieties "Sommerwind" and "Lavender Dream" at the Deutsche Rosarium in Dortmund, Germany, have led to interesting findings.

The test: Both roses were planted in parcels where roses had already been planted.

It was carefully ensured that with the removal of the old rose bushes all the reachable roots were pulled out with the plants or were pulled out during subsequent cultivation of the soil.

Well-rotted horse manure that had been composted for one year was used for the continuing improvement of the soil, with which only unsprayed straw was used as mulch. Therefore the horse manure did not contain any inhibitory chemicals that might have injured the roses. Similarly good results can probably also be achieved with commercial cow manure. The seaweed product Alginure should also prove succcessful in such instances.

• A wheelbarrow full of manure (about 127 qts [120 L]) was introduced to a parcel 43 sq ft (4 sq m) in size and was dug in well.

• Again, several months later, at planting time, a lesser amount of well-rotted manure was mixed with the soil in the planting hole.

• The plants were well tramped down and watered according to their needs.

The result: Soil exhaustion was not observed. The growth performance of the two trial varieties was entirely satisfactory in the three following years.

Like an invitation into an enchanted garden. Symmetrically arranged, yet charmingly playful. The boxwood hemispheres to the right and left of the entrance draw the eye and the steps into the garden. Entwining to crown the wall are climbing roses, from left to right "Paul Transon," "Chaplin's Pink Climber," and "New Dawn."

Buying, Planting, and
CULTURE

Get the advice of an expert when buying your first roses, for not only do roses have needs specific to their varieties, but even their color can make certain cultural measures necessary. For instance, delicate white flowers quickly turn brown in the rain. Here are the porcelainlike flowers of the shrubby Rugosa hybrid "Henry Hudson."

The first roses for one's own garden are always bought on the spur of the moment. It's a tremendous disappointment when they become diseased or bloom entirely differently from what was expected. Therefore, learn everything about a variety before you decide to grow it. Does it have healthy foliage until fall, does it bloom well, and as continuously as possible? The rose should also be right in form and color for the location you've chosen. Thus the desired location in large part determines the choice of the rose.

Tips on Buying

There are some marks of quality that you should seek.

Intact root: Only a healthy plant with an intact root can produce fast, robust growth. Make sure the roots are healthy and strong.

True to variety: When you order roses, don't agree to accept substitutions. Select your variety and insist on the one you've chosen.

Classification: Roses are distinguished as A and B quality. A rose in category A must have a well-branched root structure and three sturdy canes growing directly out of the bud union or at least a hand breadth over it. Roses of B quality have only two sturdy canes.

Appearance of the canes: The green wood of the rose cane must be smooth and firm. Soft, shrunken grooves—usually longitudinal—indicate considerable lack of water during the transport of the roses. Roses should not be dug and sold before the middle of October.

The scented shrub rose "Snow White" forms entrancing standards (see page 5). Here, one is the focal point between perennial companions like *Geranium, Hosta, Digitalis,* and *Salvia sclarea* (right).

Buying, Planting, and CULTURE

My tip: Don't buy any roses with mottled canes or injury from lack of water.

The Best Planting Time

Planting in late fall: The best planting time is from the middle of October to the first heavy frost. At this time the plants can still develop strong roots and then at the beginning of spring are ready to put out new growth as soon as nutrients and water are provided.

Planting in spring: As long as the ground isn't frozen or too wet, you can plant all winter long until spring. Don't forget to soak the roses for several hours before planting. But the roses should be in the ground by the middle of April (for proper planting, see KNOW-HOW: Planting, pages 32 and 33).

My tip: Never allow frost to reach the bare roots. This can lead to the rapid death of the plant.

Planting Container Roses

Since there are roses grown in pots, you can plant them all summer long. You can see the roses in bloom and can determine the best colors for the garden. However, because of their greater care requirements, container roses are somewhat more expensive than bare-root ones.

• Keep the roses damp in the days before planting, since they dry out quickly.

• Massive pruning is not necessary but does lead to thicker branching. Root pruning is unnecessary.

• Removing from the pot: Turn the pot and rose upside down, supporting the rose with your hand, and strike the upper rim of the pot on the edge of a table or bench. Turn the pot upright again and

The once-blooming "Hebe's Lip" is a striking hybrid, probably between *Rosa damascena* and *Rosa rubiginosa*. It has red blotches along the edges of the petals.

place the plant and earth ball in the prepared planting hole.

• Then fill in the soil, tamp it down, and water. Water frequently during the summer because the roots will still not have reached their depth.

Further Planting Measures

• Shoots from the understock must be rubbed away or cut off as soon as they appear (see KNOW-HOW: Pruning, page 43)

• When painting a rose arbor or a wall covered with roses is unavoidable, it should be done immediately after the first rush of flowering. Thus, if the roses must be cut back, the long canes of the current year may be preserved and refastened again when the painting is finished. This way you will have acceptable flowers again the next year.

• An important requirement for "garden hygiene" is the collection of fallen and diseased leaves. Spores sprout and grow on each fallen leaf and will infect the shrub all over again. You can reduce blackspot through collecting the leaves. They should be placed in the garbage and not find their way into the compost heap. Only a thermocomposter will kill the spores with the heat of rotting, to some extent.

My tip: With all repeat-blooming bedding and shrub roses, cut back the flower or flower cluster to the topmost fully developed leaves of the main cane immediately after blooming is finished.

Soil Culture

Soil cultivation is critical for healthy, lushly blooming roses in the garden. A soil with an intact, varied microflora and microfauna and abundant bacterial life is the best for roses because such soil is well aerated and has good water permeability.

<u>Hoeing:</u> Through frequent shallow hoeing, the surface of the soil is kept open and the

The once-blooming "Constance Spry" is half shrub, half climbing rose. Here it grows with campanula in front of a garden wall. It frames the cozy little spot like a canopy.

weeds destroyed. Also the gas exchange is facilitated. Whether you use a shallow hoe or a grubber depends primarily on the condition of the soil. It's enough if you stir up the soil once a month. This loosening also improves water drainage.

My tip: Don't injure the rose roots when you are hoeing because every injury stimulates the plant to production of canes from the understock.

<u>Mulch:</u> This is the term for covering the soil surface with organic material. Not only is mulch a supply for the life in the soil to process but it also hinders the rapid drying out of the soil surface by the sun and wind. The mulch layer takes up the water from downpours and prevents sludging of the upper soil layers. Mulch saves hoeing.

Suitable material: A mixture of leaves, grass, pruned branches, and compost has

Continued on page 34

Rose **KNOW-HOW**: *Planting*

The best planting time for roses is the fall. If they come right out of cold storage, you can even plant until the end of May. Here we show you step by step what to do so that everything will look rosy in your garden.

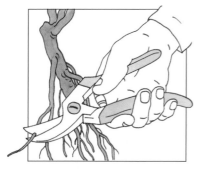

1 Planting roses.
a Remove injured roots; shorten long ones about 10 in. (25 cm).

Bare-root roses—that is, not container-grown—should be unpacked as soon as they arrive. If they cannot be planted immediately, heel them in, either in a bucket of damp sand or in soil.

1 Soil improvement: This topic is treated in detail on pages 18 to 27. A preliminary fertilizing with lime, potassium, and phosphorus is then only necessary when soil testing has indicated a deficiency. Lime and potassium should only be added sparingly. Fertilize several weeks before planting, so that the soil can "settle down." Mix fertilizer in well with the underlayers of soil.

2 Watering: Before planting, lay the roses in a tub and cover them with water for several hours. In the fall, 2 to 3 hours are enough; in the spring, it should be for 6 to 8 hours.

3 Cutting back: Before planting, prune back all canes more or less severely:
- Bedding roses to 4–6 in. (10–15 cm),
- Climbing roses up to 27 in. (70 cm), depending on how strong a grower they are,
- Shrub roses to around 12 in. (30 cm).

With roses that are shipped, cut them back very short and omit the fall pruning. The plant can be "cleaned up" in the spring.

4 Root pruning (see drawing 1a): Prune away all injured or damaged roots up to the healthy areas. Shorten healthy roots to 8–10 in. (20–25 cm) long (a hand's span).

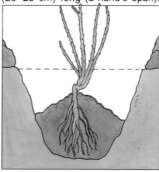

b The bud union must be 2 in. (5 cm) deep under the earth.

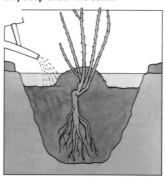

d Make a rim to hold in water, then water gently.

It's advisable to dip the roots in a slurry of mud, especially in very light soil, but it's not absolutely necessary.

5 Digging the hole: Dig the planting hole deep and wide enough so that the roots will fit perpendicularly and the bud union will lie about 2 in. (5 cm) under the surface of the soil (see drawing 1b).

6 Placing the rose: Carefully mix the planting soil with some good, well-rotted compost. Support the rose in the planting hole and add soil until the hole is firmly filled. Make sure that the soil has also gotten down in among the roots. Avoid leaving any spaces where air is trapped.

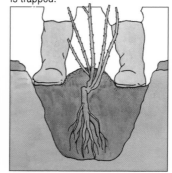

c Fill in with planting soil and press firm or tramp down.

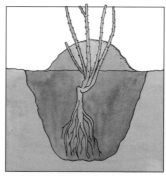

e Hill up soil to 6 in. (15 cm). Protect from frost, wind, and sun.

My tip: At first, place the rose a scant inch deeper in the hole than it's going to be finally. Afterwards, carefully draw the rose upward for that scant inch so that the roots will "stretch" straight.

7 Firming the soil (see drawing 1c): With your feet, tramp soil down well, preferably from the sides inward, to make a shallow depression to hold water. As a rule the soil is firm enough when you can pull on the rose with two fingers without pulling it out of the ground. Tread more gently with very damp soil so that it doesn't compact and thus "cement in" the plant.

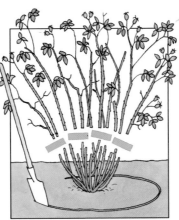

3 Transplanting roses.
a Shorten canes. Dig out generously in order to preserve the root ball.

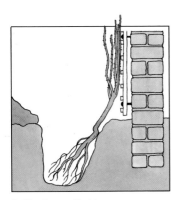

2 Planting a climbing rose.
Dig a hole 20–23 in. (50–60 cm) away from the wall; lay the roots at an angle to the trellis.

8 Watering (see drawing 1d): Next, water well. Strong sluicing serves to eliminate the air spaces in the root region but it endangers the soil structure. In well-drained soils it may be tolerated, especially in spring, but in heavy soil it is not advisable except when the water content of the soil is clearly too low at planting time.

9 Hilling (see drawing 1e): Finally, hill up good, ordinary garden

soil around the plant. Don't ever use peat!

My tip: After planting, loosen the label wire, or better, remove it entirely, so that later it doesn't girdle (strangle) the rose when the rose grows.

Planting Standard Roses

Planting rose trees is not any different in principle. They must be set in the earth at the same depth as they were in the nursery. This is easy to see. First place the stake in the hole, then plant the rose 2–3 in. (5–8 cm) away from it. For fall planting, the crown, under which the graft union of standard roses is found, should also be covered with earth. To do this you bend the trunk down, but only several weeks after planting. To keep the roots from being heaved out of the ground, hill well with soil.

Planting Climbing Roses

(see drawing 2)
With roses that are going to climb up a house wall, the planting hole should be some 20–23 in. (50–60 cm) away from the wall. The roots must point away from the house at an angle. Here also the bud union must be 2 in. (5 cm) under the soil!

b Set the rose in the new planting hole as deeply as before. Then hill up.

Transplanting Roses

(see drawing 3)
Anyone who is going to transplant an old rose should observe the following:

- Make the new planting hole large enough.
- Cut the rose back to 8–12 in. (20–30 cm).
- With vertical strokes of the spade, make a circle 16–23 in. (40–60 cm) Ø around the base of the plant. Outside this circle dig out the earth on one side; with large bushes go all the way around.
- With slanting spade strokes loosen the ball and lift it out.
- Drag heavy balls on a thick plank to the new planting hole.
- Set the rose at the same height as before, filling in with earth underneath and around the sides.
- Firm the soil well, and water.

Buying, Planting, and CULTURE

proved very successful. Also bark mulch is suitable if in spring some supplementary nitrogen fertilizer—for example, horn meal—is added at the same time. Ready-made compost is also a soil improver. But a mulch of compost must be weeded every 14 days because of the weed seeds.

This is how mulch is made:
• Very carefully remove weeds such as thistles, bindweed, stinging nettles, bunch grass, and goutweed before mulching. Bark mulch, with its rich tannin content, only has a weed-killing (herbicidal) effect on annual weed seeds.
• The thickness of the mulch should not exceed $1^{1}/_{2}$–2 in. (4–6 cm), depending on the material. Fresh grass clippings clump together readily; therefore use them $^{3}/_{4}$ in. (2 cm) thick or let them dry out for a day. Ready-made bark compost may be up to 2 in. (5 cm) thick. It's better to mulch thinner and more often.

The pale lavender blue of Lavender "Munstead," the dark *Buxus* plants, and the blue green of red cabbage allow the white of the rose "Little White Pet" to shine especially beautifully. This old polyantha rose from 1879 is grafted to a standard here.

• When the mulch layer has turned to humus, it must be mixed into the topsoil with loose, shallow hoeing. Then you can add new mulch.

My tip: Cover roses with bark mulch only after one year's growth.

Rules for Watering

Although rain water seeps away rather too quickly in sandy soils, heavier loams and especially clay are in danger of standing water. Compost and other humusy materials gradually improve the soil structure and also improve the water conduction of such soils.

Water from rain and irrigation moves from one layer of soil to the next deeper one only after the first layer has been completely saturated. The ground can thus remain dry as dust at a depth of 4 to 8 in. (10 to 20 cm), even after a long-awaited summer rain.

Don't overwater, because the leaves of the rose should not get wet, if possible. This avoids the promotion of disease.

Before watering, make a little wall of soil around the bush so that the water won't flow where you don't want it to flow. In beds of mixed plantings, make furrows for the water to run into so that it can seep in well.

Only water as necessary, then do it thoroughly. Despite the risk of occasionally muddying the soil and damaging its structure with a rush of water, irrigating or flooding is an appropriate way to avoid damage from drought without wetting the foliage. Use 5–10 gallons (20–40 L) per 11 sq ft (per sq m).

With very sandy soil, water weekly. Two days after watering, loosen the topsoil with the hoe, to provide openings for air and to conserve the soil structure.

Useful Information About Nutrients

Nutrients are necessary for the growth of the plant and must be available in the correct proportions. One distinguishes between principal nutrients (see below) and trace elements, of which plants need only very small quantities at a time. Chief among the latter are manganese, boron, zinc, copper, molybdenum, and iron.

By means of a soil test between fall and spring, but not after a fertilizing, you can discover whether the nutrient content of the soil is balanced. The procedure is to take a sample of the soil with an augur or a spade at 15 different places at a time at a depth of 12 in. (30 cm) and to take a second sample at a depth of from 12 to 23 in. (30 to 60 cm). All samples from each depth should be mixed together well, and 18 oz (500 g) each of the top soil and the under soils

Buying, Planting, and CULTURE

should be sent, in clean, labeled plastic containers, to a soil testing laboratory. With the analysis you receive a recommendation for fertilization for the desired culture.

The principal nutrients:

Nitrogen (N) is the essential driving power for growth. In excess it bloats the tissue and makes it susceptible to frost and disease (mildew). After the end of June, therefore, do not use any more nitrogen-containing fertilizers on your roses. Stop slow-release fertilizers even sooner.

Potassium (K) regulates the water content of the plants. It lowers frost-tenderness and hardens the wood, thus counterbalancing the bloating tendency of nitrogen. Do not use any pure salts of potassium but a potassium-magnesium fertilizer, which is available commercially as potash. Otherwise the balanced proportions of potassium and magnesium in the soil will be disturbed. With a handful of potash in July or August you can still increase the frost-hardiness before winter. Also, clean wood ashes are a good potassium fertilizer. However, you should never use coal ashes.

Phosphorus (P) promotes flowering and fruiting.

Magnesium (Mg) functions in leaf greening and has balancing functions in the plant's metabolism.

Calcium (Ca) regulates the pH values in the soil. Excess calcium can bind iron and thus produce chlorosis, a yellowing of the leaves. The optimum is a pH value of 6.5. In general, where limestone is the principal component of the soil, there is already enough calcium in the soil. Also, loess loams are usually well-provided with calcium. A pH measurement will give precise information, and you can take this yourself with commercially available quick tests. In fact, many soils need a maintenance liming of $1\frac{1}{2}$ to 2 oz (40 to 60 g) dolomite marl or calcium carbonate per 11 sq ft (per sq m) per year, to compensate for acid rain. With shell or algae lime use 20 percent more. In rainy regions the acidity is higher than in dry areas. Dolomite marl improves the magnesium content of the soil at the same time.

Important: Never use caustic lime. Its effect is too strong.

Lime and other fertilizers are also available commercially in granular form and so can be spread easily.

My tip: Don't spread lime and fertilizers on the flowers or, when foliage is damp, on the leaves.

Rules for Fertilizing

Basically the rule is: Don't fertilize roses for a whole year after planting, so that they can develop a good root system.

Divide fertilizer applications: It's best to apply fertilizers in several small doses. Thus you avoid sudden thrusts of nutrients, which may shock the plant.

Consider the assimilation time: According to whether you use organic or inorganic fertilizers, the nutrients become available to the roots at different times. Organic fertilizers must first be digested by the microorganisms and thus become ready and accessible for the plants. They work "according to nature," that is, continually. On the other hand, inorganic fertilizers work immediately and thus provoke shocks.

Fertilizing with mulch: If you use mulch, you should fertilize in spring, but at latest in May or June, so that the fertilizer will reach the roots in time. Also increase the nitrogen content by around 25 percent.

Fertilizers

Organic fertilizers like manure or compost "feed" the soil organisms. These slowly transform the fertilizer into available nutrients for the plant and improve the structure of the soil at the same time.

Inorganic fertilizers nourish the plant directly, but their

salts endanger the microorganisms in the soil. The soil structure can deteriorate.

Compost and Manure

Correct composting: You can put all organic kitchen waste on the compost heap, including coffee grounds.

• Always strew some loamy garden soil between the layers so that the earthworms can also produce the really valuable clay-humus complexes (see page 24).

• To increase the nitrogen content, you can later add bonemeal.

Manures suitable for roses:

• At least one-year-old or, better still, composted horse or cow manure. It contains many polyuronides, which are important for the development of long-lasting humus. Manure also supplies abundant nitrogen to the soil.

• Pig, small-mammal, and bird manures should only be used in a composted mixture.

• Those who have no access to such rural sources of manure may buy commercial dried cow manure.

How to use manure and compost:

• Roses thrive with an application of manure of $6^1/_2$ lb per 11 sq ft (3 kg per sq m) every three years. If to this you add 2 lb (1 kg) of compost per 11 sq ft (per sq m) every year, you do much to improve the soil.

• You can lay out aged compost (also bark compost) in the fall, for the root development begins in late fall.

• Compost or manure that is not fully mature, which is still producing warmth and is rich in nitrogen, should not be applied to the roses until the middle of February. Otherwise there is danger of frost injury.

My tip: Never use fresh horse manure because the escaping ammonia gas can burn the plants.

Nitrogen and Potassium Fertilizers

Horn meal slowly supplies organic nitrogen. You can spread it as early as October and let it be absorbed. A handful every 11 sq ft (1 sq m) is sufficient.

The second application may be spread from April to May—again, a handful.

Inorganic fertilizers are usually easily water-soluble and can be absorbed by the plants immediately. You begin fertilizing from the end of February. After the end of June, do not use any more nitrogen fertilizers, so as not to produce growth and also to avoid winter freezing.

My tip: It's easy to add fertilization with potash, or potassium salt (half a handful per 11 sq ft [1 sq m]), to the administration of nitrogen fertilizer. A second fertilization with potassium is recommended for July or the beginning of August.

Phosphorus Fertilizers

Through decades of application of bonemeal and superphosphate, many garden soils are provided with sufficient phosphorus, to some degree even too much.

Bonemeal and blood meal are organic fertilizers that, besides nitrogen, raise the phosphorus content of the soil.

Multinutrient Fertilizers

Complete fertilizers are obtainable as organic, inorganic, or combination organic-inorganic fertilizers. The proportions of their chief nutrients (N, P, K) are usually given on the package. The organic portion of the combination fertilizers is not very high.

Liquid Fertilizers

These work especially fast and can quickly relieve an acute nutrient deficiency. The quantities are mixed with the irrigation water according to the package label so that spraying a 1 to 3 percent solution provides about 0.1 oz (3–4 g) of nitrogen per 11 sq ft (per sq m). If the ground is too dry, you should lower the concentration.

Continued on page 40

Rose **KNOW-HOW:** *Overwintering*

The worry that frost can destroy the entire display of roses in the garden oppresses every rose fancier, but it's unfounded if you "pack" your plants correctly.

Now and then a light frost is

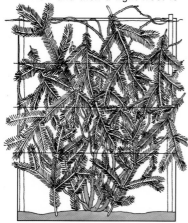

1 Roses on trellises should be covered all over the surface with spruce branches before Christmas. In addition, carefully protect the base of the plant with branches.

even good for the roses, because it makes them hardier as a result. Much more dangerous than frost are weather swings. The warming sun stimulates the resting canes of the roses to put out new growth. Then a return to cold endangers them doubly. Thus winter protection is protection not just from the cold but even more from the sun and the wind.

Preparations for Winter
Don't start the winter protection of roses before the middle of November. Before that, observe the following:

• Collect fallen leaves and burn them, because the spores of blackspot winter over in them. The leaves don't belong in the compost heap because they can infect the compost soil and thus spread disease.

• Only prune "cosmetically." Remove leaves and flowers and

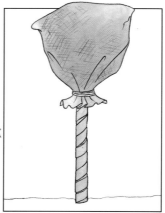

2 Older standards should be wrapped with ball burlap or sacking. Protect the bud union and crown with spruce boughs. Wrap jute sacking over all and tie.

shorten very long canes somewhat. Carefully remove this material also. Regular rose pruning is done in the spring (see KNOW-HOW: Pruning, pages 42 and 43).

3 Bedding roses. Heap base loosely with soil and also protect with branches.

Material for Covering
Pine and spruce branches serve just as well as burlap produced for the covering of bush, climbing, and cascade roses. Also, balling sacking—a loose, wide-meshed jute fabric that is used in nurseries for balling roots—can serve well as sun and winter protection.

Spruce branches have the advantage that the needles fall in the spring and thus allow sun and light to reach the canes.

Important: Don't use plastic sheeting for covering, for the sun raises the temperature under the plastic and trapped heat can result. This induces the rose to sprout and weakens its resistance. Night frosts then affect it more severely.

Overwintering Bedding, Hybrid Tea, and Shrub Roses
(see drawing 3)

• First, hill up about 8–12 in. (20–30 cm) of earth around the base of the rose. This protects the root cap and the bud union, which with proper planting lie about 2 in. (5 cm) under the soil surface (see KNOW-HOW: Planting, pages 32 and 33).

If the roses are closely planted, the soil between them should not be hoed up to use for hilling. The roots will be exposed and can be injured. It's better to use compost or soil from another part of the garden for hilling.

Important: Do not use peat for hilling. It holds water and when frozen will act like an ice pack on the roses.

• After hilling, cover the roses with spruce or pine boughs. This protects from winter sun and cold east wind.

Overwintering Climbing Roses
(see drawings 1 and 5)
- On a trellis, the climbing rose receives extra protection from spruce branches arranged like a roof. Either tie the branches to the trellis or pull them through the fastening wires. Finally, cover the base well with branches or hill it.
- Rose arbors may be covered with branches from top to bottom—scalelike, so that the water can slide down—and wrapped loosely with a cord. Jute cloth can also be used. Hill the base well.

Overwintering Standard Roses
Young Standards
(see drawing 4)
- Cut out all existing leaves and tips of canes to avoid rotting in the later-covered crown.
- With a spading fork loosen around the root region.
- Wrap the trunk up to the crown with pine boughs to protect from winter sun and formation of ice.
- Carefully bend the stem and fasten it to the ground with wire clips, forked branches, or stakes fashioned into a cross.
- Hill the graft and the crown

well with loose soil. Avoid air spaces but don't tread down the soil.

Old Standards
(see drawing 2)
- Since these will no longer bend easily, wrap the trunk loosely with sacking.
- Protect the graft and the crown with pine branches.
- Pull additional jute sacking over this and fasten it.
- In rough situations, hill the base loosely with earth and protect with additional branches.

Cascade Roses
- Even by the end of August, pull down the long canes over the crown and stabilize the bell-shaped bush with a "bellyband" (cord).
- In December, wrap the plant with jute sacking.
- After wet snows, gently shake off standards and cascade roses to avoid broken branches.

Overwintering Wild Roses
Wild roses need no additional winter protection, for in general they are winter-hardy. Naturally, some canes can die back during extreme winters. They are then cut back to healthy wood in the spring (see

5 <u>Rose arbors</u> should be covered with boughs or burlap and loosely wound. Hill the bottom.

KNOW-HOW: Pruning, page 42).
Non-frost-hardy wild roses from regions other than Europe are protected like shrub roses.

Removing Winter Protection
- At the end of March, carefully remove the spruce branches. The young new growth is easily broken.
- Hilling is removed during April, after late frosts are no longer to be expected.
- Free young standard roses from their protective coverings and let them lie there for several days. Then carefully pull them up, firm up the loosened roots, and fasten the trunk to a supporting stake.

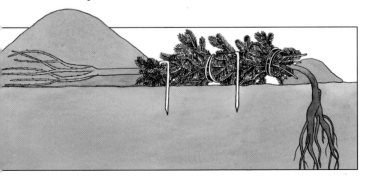

4 <u>Young standards.</u> Wrap the stem with pine boughs and carefully bend. Anchor to the ground with hooks. Hill base, bud union, and crown well with soil.

Buying, Planting, and CULTURE

Proper Pruning

Wild roses should be allowed to develop their natural forms with as little pruning as possible. All other roses are pruned in different ways according to whether they bloom once or repeatedly, or whether they are bedding, shrub, or climbing roses (see KNOW-HOW: Pruning, pages 42–43). Pruning stimulates formation of flowers and growth and is necessary for the regeneration of the rose.

"Bantry Bay" and "New Dawn," two repeat-blooming roses climbing on a house overgrown with greenery, cast a spell over this sitting area. In the foreground to the right, in yellow green clouds, lady's-mantle and hydrangea in bloom. On the left, yellow daylilies and funkia.

When to Prune?

Around April 1 is the principal pruning time; in milder regions you can begin 14 days earlier, however.

In summer shrub roses and climbers may be thinned out. This pruning immediately after flowering stimulates the development of new annual canes. With all repeat-blooming roses, faded flowers should also be removed regularly. This promotes renewed flowering.

In fall only frozen flowers or hips should be cut off.

What to Prune With?
Most suitable is a sharp pair of garden shears. For shrub and climbing roses the loppers, enlarged shears with handles 20–23 in. (50–60 cm) long, are practical. The longer lever arm vanquishes sturdy canes of 2 in. (5 cm) in diameter.

Where to Put the Prunings?
Everything that has been pruned from a rose should be carefully raked up and placed in the trash disposal. Under no circumstances should any pruned branches be placed on the compost heap. Thus you will avoid spreading fungus infection, such as mildew.

Tips for Pruning Bedding Roses
The relationship between vigor and pruning should always be balanced.
- Weak plants are cut back hard; they then develop stronger canes.
- Sturdy roses can be left an inch or so (a few centimeters) longer.
- Bedding roses that have become too tall can be cut back the next spring to "old wood," that is, to canes that are several seasons old. The rose will immediately become bushy with new shoots from its "sleeping eyes" (dormant buds), rejuvenating the entire plant at the same time.

Pruning Shrub Roses
Cutting back hard: The better a variety maintains continued blooming, the better it tolerates the hard pruning of the repeat-blooming roses: These shrub roses are pruned like the oversized bedding roses.

The "eco-cut" for once-blooming, round bushes: The old canes are used as inner supports for the bush, over which the new canes are laid every year like a cloak and only minimally shortened. But the variety must be vigorous enough so that the interior of the bush is completely covered.

Thinning is important for shrub roses with twiggy growth. This is done at the end of March or immediately after the first blooming by cutting out the canes that are older than three years. This method is appropriate for the bushes that fall apart easily, the centifolias and moss roses. Bourbon roses also respond well to it.

Pruning for rejuvenation: When after many years the bushes have slackened growth too much or have become bare in their lower regions, a radical rejuvenating pruning is appropriate. Cut all old (brown, woody) canes back to 8–12 in. (20–30 cm). Leave the annual (green) canes that come from the base. The rose will quickly become bushlike again. In some circumstances, however, this radical operation can sometimes be unsuccessful. Undertake it only at wide intervals.

Pruning Climbing Roses
The long, flowerless, whiplike canes that grow over the course of a summer are not like wild canes but are the valuable flower-bearers for the next summer. You give them shape by carefully fastening them to an arbor or a trellis. The goal in the pruning of all climbing roses is to retain as many as possible of these sturdy canes for the next year of blooming.

Development and pruning of a cane over three years:
- First year: Do not cut the long cane of the climbing rose; it should only be shortened after frost damage.
- Second year: From almost every eye of this long cane, flowers will develop on side canes. Cutting the flowers in summer will stimulate repeat-blooming varieties to the production of new flowering canes the same year. In winter, shorten all side canes to from two to four eyes, depending on their vigor; side canes of more than 23 in. (60 cm) in length can be treated as new long canes, but these should not be allowed to be situated too closely together.
- Third year: Flower-bearing branches will again grow from most stumps. Since these become smaller and weaker if you observe the same method in following years, it is recommended that you completely remove such old wood after blooming so as to promote the formation of new long canes.

Rose **KNOW-HOW:** *Pruning*

Pruning roses is not a science. If you consider that a single rose cane bud can produce three sturdy canes in succession in only one summer, you can apply your clippers with an easy mind. We'll show you how to do it step by step.

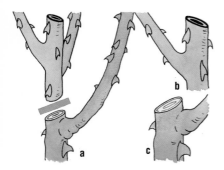

1 Cut off dead wood.
a Cut back dead wood to the base of a green shoot.
b You can recognize dead wood by its brown center.
c Healthy wood has a white or light green center.

What You Need to Know Beforehand

• The buds on the canes are called "eyes." Little red spots in the leaf axils, they are easy to recognize. The farther from the root they are, the more vigorous they are, and therefore the earlier they sprout. The lower-lying eyes "sleep" longer and need a longer time to sprout.
• "Old" wood is the term for canes several years old; "new" wood is the one-year-old growth.
• The main pruning takes place somewhere around the first of April; in fall there is merely "tidying up."
• Once-blooming roses only

flower on short canes that arise from the buds of the canes formed the previous year.
• Repeat-blooming roses also flower on the canes that develop over the summer from the canes of this year that have already flowered, and there they produce the second and third flowering.

The Correct Cut
(see drawing 4)
Roses are pruned about 4 in. (1 cm) above the eye, not too slanting! The wound and evaporation surface should be as small as possible. If a peg is left, it won't matter. It will dry and can easily be removed with the next winter pruning.

Sick or frost-damaged canes must be rigorously cut back to healthy wood. Healthy wood is recognizable by white or green pith; sick wood is brownish-colored (see drawing 1).

My tip: Only use very sharp pruners or saws. You must ensure a smooth cut, and the cane must never be crushed.

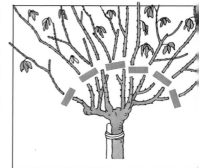

2 Pruning standard roses. Shorten to 1–2 eyes (buds) at the end of March.

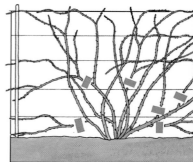

3 Pruning climbing roses. Cut out old wood and crossing canes. Shorten long canes and adjust distribution; cut short canes back to two eyes (buds).

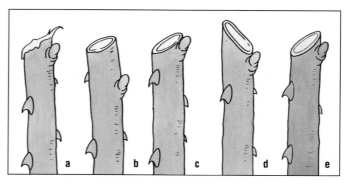

4 The right cut (e) is 4 in. (1 cm) over the eye.
Don't break off (a) or cut too high (b), too low (c), or into a leaf bud (d).

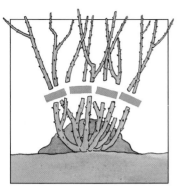

5 Pruning bedding roses. Cut canes back to 3–6 eyes.

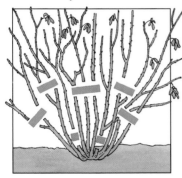

6 Thinning out shrub roses. With repeat-blooming roses remove old branches directly above the ground. Shorten the remaining ones by one third.

Bedding Roses
(see drawing 5)

Remove all weak, sick, or injured short canes and all dead wood, and cut older plants back to three to eight canes, depending on their vigor. Equalize the length of the canes so that they all have the same sap pressure.

Less vigorous varieties should be cut to two or three eyes per cane.

Vigorously growing plants of all classes—from miniature roses to hybrid teas—should have a maximum of five fully developed eyes per cane.

Shrub Roses
(see drawing 6)

Repeat-blooming shrub roses: Remove canes that are too close together or crossing. Cut back the remainder to about a third of their last-year's growth.

Once-blooming shrub roses: Prune as little as possible in winter and instead provide for careful soil cultivation and fertilizing. Thin bushes that have grown too thick by removing the oldest branches.

Climbing Roses
(see drawing 3)

Repeat-blooming climbing roses: After they bloom, remove all flowers. Cut out old, died-back wood at the base. Leave new long canes; cut back new side shoots to two to four eyes or treat canes of more than 23 in. (60 cm) as new canes, but provide for symmetrical distribution.

Once-blooming climbing roses: Treat like the repeat-bloomers but leave the short canes. With all varieties that bear hips in the fall, don't cut away the faded flowers.

My tip: If climbing roses are growing on trees, don't prune at all the first year but direct the long canes as high as possible from outside into the tree. In later years, cut out the dead wood as much as you can.

Standards and Cascades
(see drawing 2)

Standards: To keep the crown compact, don't allow the canes to branch out. Just thin all weakly growing varieties and remove aged wood. Moderately shorten "large-flowered" and "cluster-flowered" standards in late fall; at the end of March prune the bushes very short

to one to two eyes per cane. Cut back after flowering to three to four leaves.

Cascade roses: These climbing roses grafted to a standard should not be pruned at all for the first three to four years after planting, and then should only be thinned and have the oldest wood removed.

7 Removing wild canes.
a Important! Clear around the root neck; remove wild cane at the base or cut it off without leaving a stump.

b Wrong! Don't cut away above the ground, for new canes will come up from the old stump.

43

The Healthy
ROSE

Anyone who lets the garden become a home for many creatures has plenty of assistants who work for nothing to help keep roses healthy. These are the beneficial insects like the ladybug, whose larvae are particularly voracious aphid predators. Important: If possible, don't use any insecticides, because they kill the beneficial insects too.

Diseases and parasites are part of life. World-wide. You avoid them, you try to combat them, you take pains to develop intrinsic hardiness, but you can't escape them. If you accept them, you can live with them. Is it any different with roses? Roses are almost never planted because of their sturdiness but out of love for their beauty. The sensible rose lover should search out from the multitude of those available the varieties that correspond to his or her idea of beauty but are also healthy. With these roses you can avoid chemical materials entirely.

Roses on the Testing Bench

Some varieties may either lose vitality over the course of years or become strengthened by severe damage from fungus. These dynamic adaptation processes of nature cannot be influenced by human beings. Thus the evaluation of a variety is difficult and not valid for all time.

ADR Testing in Germany (ADR = Accredited German Rose) is recognized the world over as the most rigorous rose rating in the area of health. Nine test gardens in various locations in Germany test the same variety for a period of three to four years. During this time the roses may not be treated for fungus disease. Roses that receive the ADR label are considered healthy. German rose nurseries note this certificate (the ADR symbol) in their catalogues as a special distinction. In order to protect the ADR grade, it is no longer used for varieties that become increasingly more susceptible and that have carried the grade for longer than 10 years.

Growers who have a good sense for the choice of crossing partner, no longer spray the seedlings, and at the same time select carefully, have performed well with their varieties in the ADR trials in the last few years. The robust

novelties arise primarily from the crossing of disease-resistant wild species.

Prevention Is Better than Cure

Plant protection begins with setting the right plant in the right place in the ground (see pages 18–26).

• Don't plant roses in soggy ground, or else put in a drainage system.

• Don't wet the leaves when watering.

• Shallowly cultivate the soil often, or mulch.

• Remove sources of infection (fallen leaves and bits of cane) regularly; if necessary

"Chorus" is a robust cluster-flowered bedding rose with curled petals. It is a very heavy bloomer and quite healthy.

remove infected plants before winter.

• Encouraging birds and beneficial insects controls pests. Your garden should be an environment for many beneficial animals.

Keeping Off Disease and Pests

Fungus disease on roses can be combatted entirely by biological means. Light and air as well as soil cultivation are the

first steps. Only after that should you look for a suitable fungicide.

Insects can also be countered by natural means. Preying mites can be introduced against spider mites, bacilli against caterpillars, ladybugs against aphids.

In addition, there are commercially available insecticides to control biting and sucking insects and mites. However, you should employ these materials only in an emergency. Get advice from your dealer or garden center and use only products that are labeled "safe for bees" and "will not harm beneficial insects."

45

In the Rosarium L'Häy-les-Roses near Paris, the dream of rose arbors is potentiated. Here rambler roses show what they can do. From front to back, the varieties are "American Pillar," "Dorothy Perkins," "Aviateur Biériot," "Excelsa," and way at the back, "Veilchenblau."

The Healthy ROSE

To Spray or Not to Spray?
A well-known economic principle of plant protection is the so-called "damage threshold." Spraying is done only when the cost of the damage caused by a pest threatens to become greater than the cost of combatting it. As long as other factors like weather conditions or beneficial animals can keep the development of a pest under control "by nature" and don't allow it to cross this threshold, you needn't intervene. A mass increase of aphids, for instance, is often stimulated by a warm spell. The next change to cool, rainy weather, however, kills off most of the aphids. Spraying just before this cold rain would be unnecessary. It would also dispose of masses of beneficial insects that could have decimated the remaining aphids after the rain. Spraying should be a last resort.

Tips for spraying:
• Never spray on open flowers.
• Many pests and funguses attack the undersides of leaves. Therefore always spray the backs of the leaves well.
• Change spraying agents to avoid development of resistance by pests.

Make sure:
• Not to use any highly poisonous chemicals marked with T, T+, or ☠.
• To follow the product label instructions for mixing and application exactly.
• Not to breathe in any spray.
• To wear gloves and mask when working with plant protection materials.
• To keep plant sprays and chemicals in their original packages, out of the reach of children and animals, separate from food or household materials, and locked up securely.
• To keep the residues out of the ordinary trash collection. There are special dumps for toxic waste.
• To avoid spraying when children and pets are in the garden.
• To observe the important note on page 159.

Rose Diseases
The most common rose diseases are described and examples pictured on pages 50 and 51. Here are two other important diseases:

Valsa disease *(Valsa cincta, Valsa persoonii):* Death of canes. Appears almost exclusively on *Rosa hugonis* and similar early bloomers. The ends of the canes wilt; individual branches die out. Loss of the entire plant is possible. Don't leave any stubs when pruning. Don't plant near stone fruit or forsythia. Remove infected canes back to healthy wood. Disinfect pruning shears with alcohol.

Virus diseases: Reduction of flower development, weak growth, injury to chlorophyll (chlorosis). Transmitted by sucking insects or infected pruning equipment. Disinfection of knives and shears by alcohol. Infected plants should be carefully dug out and destroyed.

Rose Pests
The most common rose pests are described and illustrated with examples on pages 52 and 53.

They cause damage to the rose and its growth by living on it. Beneficial insects in turn live on these pests. The pests must always have reproduced strongly before the beneficial insects can noticeably increase. If aphids appear in subtantial numbers, then ladybugs will develop in volume as they feed on the aphids. When another factor like wet, cold weather reduces the reproduction quota of aphids, the ladybugs are quickly the lord of the field.

Comfortably leave to nature as much self-regulation as possible and don't immediately intervene drastically with the "chemical arsenal."

Additional pests on the aboveground plant parts:
• Winter moth caterpillars—recognizable by their inchworm gait—eat young canes and leaves. Collect and destroy the affected leaves and canes.
• Rose gall wasps are almost exclusively found on wild roses. During egg-laying and growth of the larva they

48

create mosslike, ball-shaped structures around the cane. The part of the cane beyond the gall usually dies back. Cut off the galls and destroy them.

• Shining leaf chafer, rose chafer, garden chafer (*Phyllopertha horticola*), and summer chafer (*Amphimallus solstitialis*) eat away the insides of the flowers.

• Pests appearing periodically are rose-leaf wasps, with holes eaten in leaves, and blossom weevils, with broken buds.

• The earwig as a beneficial insect eats plant lice; as a pest—rarely—it also eats young shoots and the inner petals of flowers.

• Snout weevils and owl caterpillars eat flower petals and cane tips.

• Rose-hip flies and rose-hip winders lay their eggs in the unripe fruit of wild roses. The larvae feed on the flesh of the fruit.

• Rabbits or deer eat rose-buds and new shoots. A small-mesh fence (at least 39 in. [100 cm] high and set 12 in. [30 cm] into the ground) keeps out rabbits. For deer, increase this fence with four to five horizontal wires to 98 in. (250 cm).

Pests in the root region:

• Nematodes live as parasites on the root tissue and cause stunted growth as well as thickening of the roots. After clearing out infested plantings, for several years plant *Tagetes patula* varieties or also pot marigolds (*Calendula officinalis*); they repel nematodes. Only then attempt a new planting.

• Voles and field and house mice gnaw on roots or bark near the ground.

Injury from Frost and Poor Culture

Chlorosis is a yellow coloring of the leaves resulting from various causes.

• Frost injury often produces the appearance of chlorosis in new canes. Such branches die back and must be cut back to healthy wood (see KNOW-HOW: Pruning, page 42).

• Iron-deficiency chlorosis is the most common form found (see picture and text, page 51).

• Magnesium deficiency produces melting, yellowish brown spots on the underleaves.

• Sogginess and bad soil aeration produce yellowing of the leaves.

• Weed-killers and winter salt on the sidewalk near roses also produce chlorosis.

• Fresh manure can produce increased chlorosis and burning of the leaves by the evaporation of ammonia. Therefore only use well-aged manure.

• Extreme dryness usually leads to the yellowing of single leaflets. Begin watering the rose generously immediately at the first appearance of this symptom.

Bondings are growth anomalies of the branch axil in which two or three canes grow flat together. They can be conditioned by heredity but usually are clearly produced by an overbalance of nitrogen fertilizer. Since they appear only infrequently, you can just prune away such portions of the plant.

Growing through of rose blooms, which means the development of buds from the center of the flower, is conditioned by the variety and is more common with old roses. The growing through with its own pedicel, on the other hand, is a curiosity rarely seen.

Injury to the rose cane through mechanical damage or the rubbing together of two canes often heals inadequately. It's better to remove injured parts so as to avoid new damage. With standards and climbing roses the entire plant may be endangered by improper tying or tying too tightly.

Water spots appear on pink, bright red, orange, and white flowers, but seldom on yellow ones. They appear after long periods of wetness or when dew cannot evaporate.

Burning of the petals almost always occurs in the dark-red varieties, which barely reflect the sunlight that shines on them and, as a result, convert it largely to heat.

The Healthy ROSE

Rose Diseases

Roses are frequently attacked by fungus diseases. There are ways to combat them.

Spot Anthracnose
(Marssonina rosea)

Damage: Usually angular-edged, irregular black spots on the leaves. Heavy leaf drop.

Cause: Infection on leaves and ground in cold, wet weather.

Prevention: Sufficient fertilization in May/June. Spraying, for instance with Neudo Vital (6²/₃ Tbs to 10 qt [100 mL to 10 L] water), Bioblatt-Mehltau-mittel (1 Tbs to 10 qt [15 mL to 10 L] water) or horsetail extract (made by steeping equisetum stems in water).

Treatment: Spraying with appropriate fungicide, depending upon growth, at about 10- to 14-day intervals with varying chemicals.

Black Spot
(Diplocarpon rosae, Apiosporium salicinum, Fumago vagans)

Damage: Shiny, lacquered-looking droplets with black fungus field, frequently among canes that have been attacked by aphids or scale.

Cause: Aphids and scale excrete sugar-containing juice (honeydew), which is colonized by the black spot fungus.

Prevention and Treatment: Spray the rose with cold water, soft soap solutions, or insecticide.

Powdery Mildew
(Sphaerotheca pannosa var. rosae)

Damage: White, floury, easily wiped-off deposit on all young plant parts, primarily on leaves, ovary of the bud, as well as flowers and canes. At first only slightly wavy, glassy leaf spots. Clear failure to thrive of affected canes and blossom clusters. Leaves are deformed but usually do not drop. Wood does not mature, becomes vulnerable to frost.

Cause: Infection with powdery mildew spores from one-sided fertilizing, too little air circulation, heat.

Prevention: Choose a well-ventilated location, fertilize with low-nitrogen. In fall, prune back affected canes to healthy wood and destroy cuttings. In spring, prune bushes to provide circulation. Do not overfertilize.

Treatment: Depending upon growth, spray with fungicide every 10 to 14 days—also on undersides of leaves.

Downy or False Mildew
(Peronospora sparsa)

Damage: Soft, grayish white moldy area on undersides of leaves, later brownish to reddish spots. Some leaf drop.

Cause: Infection with mildew spores during continued hot, humid weather, especially in late summer in locations protected from wind.

Prevention and Treatment: Choose airy locations. Collect fallen leaves and destroy them.

Black spot

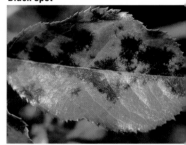

Spot anthracnose

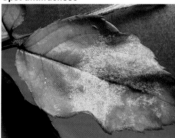

Powdery mildew

Downy mildew

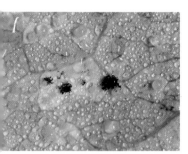

Rust

Iron chlorosis

Canker

Botrytis

Rose Rust
(Phragmidium mucronatum)

Damage: In summer, small orange-red spore deposits on the undersides of leaves; on the uppersides little yellowish leaf spots. In fall, black winter spores on the leaf undersides. Leaf drop in the consequent debilitation of the plant.

Cause: Infection by rust spores in warm weather, also during drought; epidemic-like but species-specific.

Prevention: Choose airy locations, sufficient potassium fertilization. Destroy spore carriers. Aerate the soil.

Treatment: Apply rust control sprays; vary the chemicals. Also spray healthy neighboring roses.

Iron-deficiency Chlorosis
(Jaundice, greensickness of leaves)

Damage: Yellow coloration of the young leaves; only the leaf veins remain green at first and form a fine green network in the yellow leaf.

Cause: Too much lime in the soil, keeping the iron necessary to form chlorophyll in the plant from being taken up.

Prevention: Good soil aeration, balanced fertilizers. Addition of humus.

Treatment: Adjust for the missing nutrients; create good soil conditions.

Canker
(Coniothyrium wernsdorffiae and others)

Damage: Reddish brown, often slightly sunken spots in the eye area, usual on canes from the preceding year. The affected canes die back.

Cause: Soggy soil, unbalanced fertilizing. Often affects shrub and climbing roses.

Prevention: Drainage and good soil aeration. Fertilizing less promotes soil life.

Treatment: Remove affected canes and destroy. Treat any wounds with wound paint. Improve location.

Botrytis Disease
(Botrytis cinerea)

Damage: Balling of buds and flowers after rainfall, dropping of buds, rotting buds and flowers, spotted canes. Mouse-gray moldy deposits (not always visible). Damping off of young seedlings. Considerable diminution of flowers and vigor.

Prevention: Good air circulation, balanced fertilizer.

Treatment: Provide for better air circulation. Suspend nitrogen fertilization; fertilize with potassium. Remove affected plant parts. Fungicide sprays are only recommended with seedling beds.

The Healthy ROSE

Rose Pests

A pest attack on your roses isn't always a reason to reach for the chemical arsenal.

Leaf Miner
*(Nepticula anomalella,
Nepticula centifoliella,* and others)
<u>Damage:</u> Clearly visible traces of gnawing on the upper surface of the leaves in the middle layer of the leaf. Mostly it is older leaves that are affected, which then fall off.

<u>Cause:</u> A leaf miner moth lays its eggs in the leaf. The larvae feed on the leaf tissue.

<u>Prevention and Treatment:</u> Gather affected leaves as soon as possible and put them in the trash. Provide nesting sites and water for birds.

Rose Leafhoppers
(Typhlocyba rosae)
<u>Damage:</u> Mosaiclike, usually angular, white-spotted fine stipples on the upper surface of old leaves. Considerable sucking damage, diminished growth. Possible spread of virus. Primarily on climbing roses on warm house walls or in warm, dry locations.

<u>Cause:</u> Whitish, light green, springing leafhoppers, slenderly triangular, suck along the ribs on the undersides of the leaves. Problem of location.

<u>Prevention:</u> Improve location. Provide nesting and water for birds.

<u>Treatment:</u> Spray with appropriate insecticide, using one the least damaging to beneficial insects as possible, but only if infestation is severe.

Thrips
(Thrips fuscipennis and others)
<u>Damage:</u> Small, silvery, usually darkly bordered spots on leaves and petals; buds open poorly and can be deformed. Possible virus infection.

<u>Cause:</u> Sucking damage. Huge population explosions in heat ("thunderstorm bugs"). More common in locations that are too warm and dry. In recent years a new thrip species from California has done severe damage.

<u>Prevention and Treatment:</u> Choose better location. Cut off affected buds and destroy.

Spider Mites
Also "Red Spider"
(Tetranychus urticae)
<u>Damage:</u> Uppersides of leaves finely stippled, undersides delicately webbed with heavy infestation. Later the leaves turn brownish, growth stops, and eventually the leaves fall.

<u>Cause:</u> The spider mites, which are not insects but are web spinners, are scarcely visible to the naked eye. They live on the undersides of the leaves and suck the juices. They love warmth and dryness.

<u>Prevention:</u> Avoid hot, sunny locations in front of south walls. Provide good watering.

<u>Treatment:</u> Since there are no acaricides in small packages,

Leaf miner

Rose cicada

Thrips

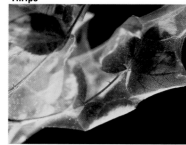

Spider mites

Scale

Rose aphid with eggs

Rose cane borer

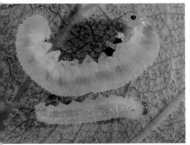

Rose leaf roller

try something like 13$^1/_3$ Tbs (200 mL) Neudosan in 10 qts (10 L) water.

Scale
(Eulecanium corni, Aulacaspis rosae)

Damage: Mother and offspring are found on one- and two-year-old canes, also on leaves. Development of black spot and failure to grow.

Cause: Too dry a location. Scale primarily attack climbing roses that are sheltered from rain by walls or roofs.

Prevention: Choice of proper location or good watering.

Treatment: Spray with paraffin or white oil. These cover the scale so that they can no longer breathe.

Aphids
(Macrosiphon rosae and others)

Damage: Sucking damage at the ends of canes, buds, and undersides of young leaves to the point of deformity. Fewer flowers, rust infestation. Possible virus infection.

Cause: Too much nitrogen fertilizer, hot location, warm and dry weather.

Prevention: Provide good ventilation. Apportion nitrogen fertilizer carefully. Protection is provided by birds, ladybugs, and lacewings.

Treatment: First squash any winged aphids as well as the colonies, but spare beneficial insects. Spray with a soap solution or fresh stinging nettle broth (2.2 lb to 10 qt [1 kg to 10 L] water). Use chemical controls only when absolutely necessary. Use materials that do not harm bees.

Cane Borer
(Ardis brunniventris and *Monophadnus elongatus)*

Damage: Individual cane tips wilt. Loss of the cane. Affects almost all the large-flowering roses, occasionally also floribundas and wild roses. Cane borer sometimes occurs epidemically.

Cause: The egg of the backwards-boring cane borer is laid in the tips of young canes. The larvae bore into the cane from above and eat their way down. The eggs of the forward-boring cane borer are laid on the leaf stem. The larvae then bore into the cane and move upward through the pith.

Prevention and Treatment: Cut wilted canes back to healthy wood; kill the approximately $^1/_2$-in. (1–1.5 cm) in length larvae. Provide nesting and water for birds.

Rose Leaf Roller Wasp
(Blennocampa pusilla)

Damage: Rose leaves are rolled like cigars. Decrease in assimilation.

Cause: Larvae in rolled leaves in May, primarily in modern bedding roses, rarely in wild roses. Pupation in soil in July.

Prevention and Treatment: Gather fallen leaves immediately; place in trash.

Propagating and
BREEDING

*Decorative hips, here of **Rosa moyesii**, are still undervalued by many rose lovers, although they adorn shrub roses and many wild roses for months at a time. Hips occur in an astonishing variety of forms. And, not least, they are also the bearers of the roses' seeds.*

H ave you ever had the experience of a cut rose forming roots in a vase? Then you realize that you needn't lose that lovely flower forever. And if the rose stem that has shown new life in the vase should one day produce its first flower in the garden or a pot, your triumph is great. Someone who is more interested in "transplanting" can also graft his or her roses, that is, place eyes from a hybrid tea rose on wild rose stock. And someone who doesn't mind a little expense can breed his or her own varieties.

Propagation

Roses can be propagated sexually (generatively) or asexually (vegetatively).

In generative propagation—the basis of every cross—the egg cell in the flower is fertilized by pollen and a seed is produced. The combination of genetic traits makes possible the development of a new individual.

In vegetative propagation roses can be propagated by means of layering, slips, hardwood cuttings, and bud grafting.

Root Cuttings, Runners, and Cuttings
On KNOW-HOW pages 58 and 59 these propagation options are explained in detail.

Root cuttings are the surest way of propagating self-rooted (that is, not grafted) roses. *Rosa rugosa, Rosa x rugotida, Rosa gallica,* and some centifolias even form runners that can be cut off.

Layering: With grafted plants, which are situated on a

Among repeat-flowering roses it is not uncommon in late fall for the last flowers, buds, and even hips to be surprised by hoar frost, all at the same time.

Propagating and BREEDING

The shrub rose "München" was grown in 1940 by Kordes and has since become a rarity in the rose garden. It is no longer obtainable commercially.

root of a genetically different species, you can root part of a cane by bending it down to the ground so that it can take root there. This is most suitable for long-caned varieties with over-hanging growth habits.

<u>Hardwood or green cuttings</u> can be placed in a sterilized potting medium or alternatively in garden soil (in semi-shade, to avoid heat pooling). Put a preserve jar over the cutting. Later, plant with "root ball."

My tip: All newer varieties are protected by copyright.

You may propagate them for your private use, but they may not be sold.

Grafting
See KNOW-HOW page 59.

Suitable stock are wildings of *Rosa canina* because they possess good frost-hardiness.

• For root grafting, only one-year-old seedlings (3–5 in. [8–12 cm] in diameter) are used; for standards, on the other hand, two- to four-year-old plants with a single, smooth cane about 59 in. (1.5 m) tall are used.

• Only one eye is placed at the root neck; on the standard, two eyes are situated opposite each other at the height of about an inch (several centimeters).

Breeding Your Own Roses

Anyone who wants to breed successfully should not only master the technology but also learn in detail about the varieties and their characteristics so as to be able to choose the best partners for hybrids.

Pollination

About a day before the petals open, they are carefully removed with tweezers, along with all the stamens. Do not injure the stigmas, for they are ready to receive the pollen.

- Take the pollen from the desired male variety with a fine-haired brush or your finger and convey it to the stigma of the female variety.
- This flower is then covered with an aluminum foil or tinfoil cover so that no fertilization by any other agent may take place.
- Provide the flower with a numbered tag. Male and female varieties, number, and date of pollination are entered in a breeding log.
- After three days remove the cover so that no mold will develop under it. The stigma is no longer receptive.

The Hips

The ripening hips have a thin, waxy covering, like apples, which is destroyed with touching. Hip rot can set in. Therefore, when crossing, grasp only the sepals.

- In December, when they are yellowish orange or red, harvest the ripened hips: Remove the seeds and clean them by washing, carefully rubbing, and sieving.
- Treat with a disinfectant to prevent mold (available from a specialty dealer). Bathe the seeds in the solution, allow them to dry, and plant immediately.

Sowing

A small greenhouse is good for sowing because there you can protect the plants against frost and keep them under better control.

- Sow the seeds in a seedbed with loose planting medium kept evenly damp or in a flat, spaced at intervals of $\frac{1}{2}$–1 in. (1–3 cm) shallowly in rows, with 4–8 in. (10–20 cm) between them. Press in lightly and barely cover with planting medium or sand. Label the seed rows with the breeding numbers.
- The seeds remain for two months at about 7° to 11°F (4°–6°C) until germination. If germination succeeds in a mild winter before the middle of February, enough light must be provided.
- Increase the temperature at the beginning of sprouting: 36° to 43°F (20°–24°C) by day and 18°F (10°C) at night. Raising at cooler temperatures delays the onset of flowering.
- From the end of May, transplant only healthy plants with root balls into the sunny planting bed. There they stay for about three years, growing on their own roots, to prove themselves.

Selection is important now: Remove plants that are sick or do not bloom satisfactorily.

Mutations, or Sports

Rarely, yet continually, new genetic deviations arise spontaneously in nature, so-called mutations or sports. If they occur in a bud, they can imprint and influence a new shoot.

As a rule, they express themselves in a single characteristic—for example, a color. Thus there appeared on the red floribunda rose "Joseph Guy" a cane with a bright pink flower. The grafts from the eyes of this cane always bloom bright pink. Thus was born a new variety, sufficiently constant, that corresponded exactly with the original variety in all characteristics except color. It was named "Frau Astrid Späth" and its discoverer—the Späth nursery—was allowed to call itself its "breeder."

Besides color mutations, changes in growth form appear relatively often: an unusually long cane will suddenly appear in low-growing varieties. Thus climbing roses can arise from bedding roses as "climbing sports." They are usually not very successful in our temperate climate, but they thrive well in more southern areas.

Rose **KNOW-HOW**: *Propagating and Grafting*

Make two or more from one. Here you'll see how to propagate roses through root cuttings, layering, green cuttings, or bud grafting, called "budding." Success will reward those who work clean. Then you can report with pride that this rose was not simply bought but was produced with your own hands.

1 Layering. Anchor the cane in the ground at the deepest point; cover over 8 in. (20 cm) of the cane.

2 Cuttings. a) Cut off cleanly a 6– to 8–in. (15–20 cm) length of cane underneath the eyes (buds). Remove all leaves except the topmost two.

Propagation Through Root Cuttings, Layering, Green Cuttings

Root cuttings: In spring cut off a sturdy root, divide it into pieces 2–3 in. (6–8 cm) long, on which the secondary roots have been left if possible, and cover shallowly with soil. Only suitable for self-rooted roses.

Layering (see drawing 1): In spring bend down a longer cane, fasten it in the ground, and cover 8 in. (20 cm) with soil. The cane tip must be showing. Especially suited to long-caned varieties with trailing growth habit.

Green cuttings: Their best time is June/July. The rose branches are just right then—not too young and soft, but still not too woody.

• Prepare the growing medium —loose garden soil or well-rotted compost (both should be as low in nutrients as possible) mixed with the same quantity of washed river sand and steamed (heated wet to 180°F [100°C]) so that seeds and weed seeds are killed. About three weeks later place the medium in somewhat deeper planting flats or flower pots. Keep loosened and

b) Stick the cutting in rooting hormone and poke it into the potting medium up to the base of the leaves.

damp, but not wet. You can also buy a ready-made medium such as perlite.

• Prepare cuttings (see drawing 2a): Cut off as much healthy cane as necessary and shorten to three to five eyes. Remove all leaves except the top two sets.

• Planting (see drawing 2b): First dip each cutting in rooting powder (available in stores and garden centers). Then stick the cuttings into the rooting medium about 2 in. (5 cm) apart, slightly at an angle, right up to the base of the leaves, press in, and water.

• Care: Cover the cutting container with a plate of glass; aerate from time to time. Place in a bright but not sunny place. If roots have formed after six weeks, transplant into a somewhat more nourishing garden soil or a compost-potting soil mixture in pots. For overwintering, set the pots in a cold frame or plant the cuttings outside and protect from frost with pine branches.

Grafting

Bud grafting has proven best with roses. In this procedure the eye of the desired variety is introduced behind the bark at the root neck of a wilding, but for standard roses high up on the wand on which the crown will later form.

First step: Plant wilding suitable for grafting (see page 56) in spring or fall in the spot where they are to grow, 8 in. (20 cm) apart, in rows each 27 in. (70 cm) apart.

Second step: Budding is done in July/August. On the day of grafting, cut scions, remove leaves (leave a leaf stem slightly less than $1/4$ in. [0.5 cm] long), remove thorns, label, and place in water. (Or keep fresh in the refrigerator wrapped in a damp cloth up to three days.)

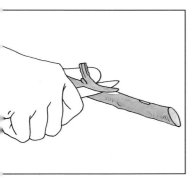

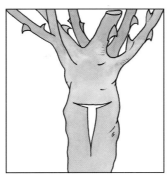

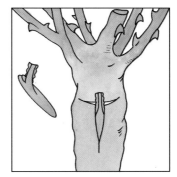

3 <u>Grafting.</u> **a) Cut a piece of stem with leaf bud from the scion, making a shallow cut in the direction of growth.**

b) With the budding knife cut a long T in the bark of the grafting stock.

c) Shove the sliver of bark with the scion eye (bud) under the two loosened wings of bark.

<u>Third step:</u> Uncover the root neck of the stock plant, wipe with a clean cloth, and bend all to one side. Always prepare only as many root necks as you can graft in one hour. Do not make the cut in the direction of prevailing winds!

<u>Fourth step:</u> Sharpen the grafting knife (available in specialty stores) well and dip it into boiling water so that it is germfree. Cleanliness is important for the growth of the bud.

<u>Fifth step:</u> The placing of the bud eye must go quickly. Therefore on the exact spot on the scion, using the grafting knife, cut out the eye, together with a sliver of bark about

4 <u>Runners from wild roses.</u> **With a sharp spade cut off the runner and plant in the desired spot.**

1-in. (3-cm) long, as shallowly as possible along the direction of growth. Then loosen the chip behind the bark from above and remove it (see drawing 3a). Use the eyes on the scion from top to bottom.

<u>Sixth step:</u> Make a T cut in the neck of the root of the wilding with the grafting knife (see drawing 3b).

<u>Seventh step:</u> With the grafting knife loosen both flaps of bark and push in the bark sliver with the bud eye from above. Whatever sticks up above the T-cut should be cut off, so that the eye and the bark sliver disappear under the bark (see drawing 3c).

<u>Eighth step:</u> Wrap it all firmly with raffia or grafting tape, leaving the eye itself free (see drawing 3d).

<u>Ninth step:</u> Hill all the grafted plants so that they don't dry out. They will overwinter this way. Standards are staked again.

<u>Tenth step:</u> Loosen the wrappings after six weeks by making a cut on back side so that they will not strangle the plant as it grows thicker. The scion bud has grown in by then and overwinters dormant on the plant.

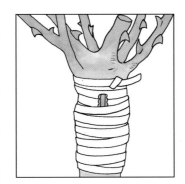

d) Wrap the whole thing firmly with raffia or bast, leaving the eye free. Or wrap with grafting tape.

<u>Eleventh step:</u> The following spring, cut off the entire crown of the stock plant a scant $\frac{1}{2}$ in. (1 cm) above the graft with a single, clean cut. Cut off sprouting wild shoots so that all the strength goes into the grafted shoot.

Designing with
ROSES
Transform Your Own Garden

*No queen without a royal household!
Underline the charm of your roses with
gorgeous companion plantings.
Or design with your roses themselves—
be it on an arbor, a pergola, or a trellis.
Let them bloom and ramble!*

Fragrant flower carpet with "Bonica '82" and campanulas. A modern cluster-flowered bedding rose with nostalgic charm and good health.

Designing with
ROSES

The capacity of climbing roses for creative feats is astonishing. This dome completely overgrown with "Alexandre Girault" at L'Häy-des-Roses near Paris can inspire anyone to the bold use of climbing roses. But enchanting garden scenes can also be created with bedding or shrub roses.

The word "garden" means an enclosed area, set off and protected from "wild" nature for cultivating useful, life-supporting plants. When it acquired shape—square, rectangular, circular, oval—human beings began to "design." The proportions became important. They had relativity to the human being.

The art of gardening makes vividly clear the powerful spiritual revolution of the Enlightenment from regimented thinking to free, responsible personality development: On the one hand, the feudal baroque castle parterre with its stiff control of the plantings and, on the other, the English landscaped park with its feeling for an apparently chaotic principle of natural order express the periods' differing views of life. The mental attitude toward dealing with nature is revealed. Diametrically opposed to the principle of control and power stand the capacity for empathy, gentleness, and concern for life. The art of gardening moves between these poles even today, under much different circumstances.

An interesting synthesis of geometric order and exuberant liveliness developed with much imagination at the beginning of this century, especially in English gardens. Within formally designed gardens the plants are given the freedom to unfold to their natural beauty unhindered by pruning or regimentation and are thus allowed to become "lively" in form. This tension relationship symbolizes "tolerance." Thus every garden reflects the personality of its owner and planner. It's rewarding to make the rose part of the design.

When Flowering Begins

Rose varieties never bloom all at the same time. There are four periods when flowering begins:

In May, early-blooming wild roses like *Rosa hugonis* or *Rosa pimpinellifolia* or shrub roses like "Nevada" and "Marguerite Hilling" begin flowering. Then some early climbing roses like "Gruss an Zabern," "Mme Sancy de Parabère," and "Gloire de Dijon," appear.

The first half of June sees the flowering of most wild roses, ground-cover roses, climbing roses, once-blooming shrub roses, and old roses.

During the second half of June most of the American wild roses, all large-flowered and cluster-flowered bedding roses, miniature roses, as well as repeat-blooming shrub roses and ground-cover roses come into flower.

At the beginning of July come the small-flowered, profusely flowering climbing roses like "Excelsa" and "Dorothy Perkins"; ground-cover roses like "Immensee," "Heidekönigin," "The Fairy," and "Palmengarten Frankfurt." In

An architectural garden in which the loose form of the roses achieves a strictly symmetrical visual effect through the use of boxwood enclosures.

Designing with ROSES

addition to the continuing blooming of bedding roses, "Mlle Cécile Brunner" and similar Chinese hybrids come along with their flowers.

These blooming periods are valid for all the mild-climate regions of North America. The other regions must reckon with a delay of one to three weeks, depending on their situation. Closer to summer, the annual variations become less.

Color and Structure

Colors are perceived very subjectively—and differently in youth than in age. Our color sense is also influenced by the spirit of the times and by fashion. Strong color contrasts express energy. Colors can be harmonious with each other or strike a note of excitement. While the everblooming roses continue their color themes throughout the summer, the accompanying plantings contribute the major or minor chords. So you can "compose" your own completely personal planting.

Structure: As the music is influenced by the tonal color of the instrument, so plant combinations are characterized, not only by the color of the flowers, but also by the lines and structure of the flower, leaves, and canes. The simple flower of a wild rose makes entirely different claims from the double, rounded flowers of a centifolia rose or the elegant spiraled form of a hybrid tea.

Therefore you want to pay attention not only to the flowers but also to the different leaf forms, color of green, and surface structure of the rose foliage and the accompanying plants. It pays to examine carefully and try things out.

A Garden for Roses

An architectural garden with beds and geometric boxwood borders can accommodate many different rose forms.

• Miniature roses are suitable for raised beds, so that the gems are closer to the eye.

• Cluster-flowering roses and hybrid teas fill out geometric areas, form beds.

• Standards or cascade roses on a flat area are outstanding points of focus and can mark avenues or corners.

• Climbing roses can be used for arbors, cones, columns, and for decorating pergolas and gazebos.

Design Elements

You'll find some additional design inspiration from the KNOW-HOW section on pages 66 and 67. The following examples are particularly good for climbing roses.

The pergola usually forms a connection between parts of a building, covers a pathway, or marks a boundary, or it might only be a place for a bench.

The rose festoon is a special form of pergola. Its size should be taken into consideration when you choose the variety.

Gazebos and canopies are similar to the arbor or the pergola. They offer protection and create a cozy atmosphere.

Garden lamps covered with roses lose their stiffness. The long canes often spread out over them like elegant umbrellas.

Trellises can be used freestanding as "room dividers" or be attached to walls to beautify them.

House walls cannot be covered without trellises. For covering surfaces the canes should be attached in a fan shape.

Walls that possess their own decorative value because of their structure, and thus should not have their surfaces covered with roses, are impressively enlivened with a climbing rose that spins a loose web of just a few canes over one corner or in an angle. For climbing roses that will hang over walls and down embankments, it is preferable to use the soft-caned rambler varieties.

Balconies over a veranda are notably enhanced by vigorous climbing roses that master these heights.

The Natural Garden

The "ecogarden" requires a certain minimum size and is controlled by the location situation as it exists. In sunny conditions this garden includes native wild roses—in unpruned free form—accompanied by pine trees, junipers, and native wildflowers like

wild bellflower, salvia, marjoram, thyme, and chicory. In urban areas the wild rose should not be objected to, even for natural gardens, on the basis of its foreign origins, especially if its hips are gladly eaten by the native birds.

The Landscaped Home Garden
Here the outspreading shrub and climbing roses have found an additional habitat. They are good "room" builders. The most natural climbing support for the rose is the tree. Wild roses, for example, will grow high into evergreen trees. Such "rose trees" must allow some

A cheerful perennial garden with roses invites freer development of the personalities of the plants. Pleasantly harmonizing with each other are the roses "Schneewittchen," "Leverkusen," and "Prosperity" with *Lysimachia punctata*, *Alchemilla mollis*, *Helichrysum*, *Anthemis*, *Inula*, and other perennials.

light to penetrate. Besides pines, suitable trees are older larches, locusts, or bizarrely shaped fruit trees.

Large gardens can be divided into various charming small areas and cozy corners by means of shrub roses, which can be planted in groups or as solitary bushes. Old and English roses could have been made for this use. Their enchanting flowers provide delight mostly with their color and scent.

My tip: Don't let roses climb on birches. These shallow-rooted trees create too much root competition.

Rose **KNOW-HOW:** *Designing with Roses*

"Anything goes, if it works"—it's exciting to design creatively with color and structure, even in the smallest garden. You need to look for suitable background and companion plants for the roses, which themselves already offer a variety of colors, flower forms, and growth habits. Roses and their companions should be harmonious or at least compatible with each other, but, on the other hand, exciting contrasts can heighten their effects considerably.

Design Tips

• With bedding roses or hybrid teas, always put at least three plants of one variety together.

• Consider the height to which plants will grow when choosing varieties.

• Combine flower and leaf colors that go with each other. Placing colors that are too vivid next to each other can also destroy harmony.

1 Rose arbors. Tie canes securely to the framework.

2 A trellis is fastened to the wall with spacers.

• In "tone-on-tone" compositions, the roses, not the companion planting, should set the tone.

• Pay attention to the flower and leaf structures in the choice of the roses' companions.

• As sun lovers, roses always need enough distance from high trees. These can still offer protection from cold winds, however.

• Especially suitable neighbors for roses are perennials like some dwarf shrubs and subshrubs, which are often classed with the shrubs, such as beard tongue, sages, lavender, or veronica species.

• Blue goes well with all rose colors.

• Quiet backgrounds are offered by dark evergreens, green ivy, or blue clematis.

Designing with Climbing Roses

Climbing roses enhance house walls, walls, fences, and many other surfaces. As a rule they need a support—for instance, a pergola or a trellis.

Rose arbors (see drawing 1): They emphasize an entrance or a special sitting area. Climbing roses must first reach height vertically be-

fore you can lay them horizontally over the arbor. Tie flexible canes on or pull them carefully through the crossbars. They will hold through their own tension.

Trellis (see drawing 2):

• Fasten it to the house wall at a distance of at least 1 in. (3 cm). A generously spaced system of rectangles made with square wood strips is practical for fastening. Spaces should be 47 in. (1.2 m) vertically and 28 in. (0.7 m) horizontally. The trellis can also be fastened to the wall in a rhomboid pattern.

• Distribute long canes over the trellis either flat or diagonally. They should not cross if possible. Of course you can also train them up in extremely formal horizontal levels (espaliering). If they are stuck between the wall and the trellis in time, tying is not necessary.

• If you use wire for fastening, it should be thickly insulated with plastic; otherwise, the danger of

3 Rose pyramid. Bamboo stakes are anchored deep in the ground, tied together at the top.

frost getting to the roses is increased because of the conductivity.

Pyramids (see drawing 3):
So that they will bloom from top to bottom, the long canes should only be trained up in gradual layers. Therefore they are laid around in a spiral and fastened. This also holds true for covering a pillar. With three or four climbing roses planted evenly around the pillar or pyramid, you can obtain uniformity.

Fence (see drawing 4):
Tie the canes on in a fan shape or horizontally. The roses will then grow in stories.

Practical Tips

Tying: Keep the current year's arching canes as horizontal as possible so that they will bloom especially heavily the next summer. With ramblers you can also let them hang down.

Materials: Good for tying are coconut string, basket willow (somewhat difficult to handle), soft insulated wire (not too stiff to pull), adjustable hooks, and plastic ties (reusable). Raffia is not suitable.

Pruning: This is especially important for arbors, pillars, and pyramids, since the vertical-growing canes bloom mainly in the upper regions the following year and are bare at the bottom. By pruning back in stages, you can balance this effect to some extent (see KNOW-HOW: Pruning, pages 42 and 43).

Designing with Shrub Roses

Solitary plantings of shrub roses are particularly effective eye-catchers, which divide the garden into individual rooms. When you make your choice, consider whether you prefer once-blooming or repeat-blooming varieties.

Designing with Standards

Cascade roses work because of their bell shape. Therefore they should always be freestanding. When planting a row of them (avenue), be careful with the distances between them.

Standard roses are an interesting design tool for accenting the geometric shapes of formal gardens.

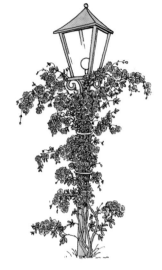

5 **Training roses up and out.** Canes of a climbing rose are directed along a garden lamppost and bound at widely spaced intervals.

Designing with Bedding and Miniature Roses

• For beds, don't choose varieties that grow too high.

• Cluster roses create a big color effect.

• The individual flowers of the large-flowered hybrid teas are always an attraction.

• In the strictly formal garden, border the rose bed with small boxwoods or a germander hedge; in the natural garden, make use of the variety of the companion plants.

• Give miniature roses, with their tiny flowers, a good, visible location—that is, plant at eye level if possible in a raised bed or terrace.

4 **Rose fence** with climbing roses. Distribute the canes and fasten while they are still flexible.

The Small Garden
Smaller shrub rose forms and, of course, hybrid tea and cluster roses gain significance here because, with their more architectural shapes, they help structure the space and yet save it.

Even a small clipped hedge offers nesting possibilities for some songbirds. For small gardens, small-flowered roses with lower growth habits, down to the polyanthas and the miniature roses—the latter even in hanging pots or baskets—are recommended.

Also, you should not forget the climbing roses, which save garden space by growing upward.

Old Gardens—New Roses
More frequent than the need to plan a new garden is the wish to change an established one. Only a few trees and shrubs will ornament the garden for a long time. Many plants must be relinquished after eight to ten years. The removal of a hedge boundary opens up the shape of the garden and brings light and sun into it: Here is a place for roses.

For trailing through trees, ramblers surpass all climbing varieties. To the left, "Rambling Rector"; to the right, "Kiftsgate."

68

Designing with ROSES

Roses and Shrubs

The planting of roses with shrubs, perennials, and annuals is exciting, but it also produces ecological and cultural problems. Roses love open, well-aerated soil, are allergic to the root networks of other plants, and use more nutrients than most of the neighboring plants.

You should follow these basic rules when planting roses and shrubs together:

• A high shrub belt in the north and east of the garden offers the roses protection

"Excelsa," a very luxuriantly blooming climbing rose, once a year changes this garden wall into a dazzling sea of flowers.

from cold winds and acts very well as a background.

• Allow enough distance from large shrubs when planting roses, because roses love sun and light.

• Coordinate the colors of flowers of shrubs and roses that bloom at the same time.

• Colored flowers of shrubs that bloom at the same time as

roses will take away from the roses' color.

• Consider carefully the size of the shrub so you won't have to prune it constantly.

• Take into consideration the location requirements of the shrub.

My tip: Mountain laurel and rhododendron are not suitable for combining with roses. Also, climbing plants like knotweed *(Polygonum aviculare)*, bittersweet, and wisteria can endanger the rose with their strong growth. Thus it's better to avoid them altogether.

Evergreens

The dark green of the evergreens' needles pleasantly brightens the colors of bedding roses and shrub roses planted in front of evergreens.

• In larger gardens, you can use high-growing shrubs like fir, larch, spruce, pine, cedar, and Douglas fir as backgrounds. Some forms of the pine are also suitable for smaller gardens. They go very well with wild roses.

• Medium-high evergreens can work well as background, but also as companions to roses singly or in groups: yew, dwarf pine, and juniper are appropriate, as are hemlock fir, arborvitae, and Japanese cypress.

• Low-growing evergreens can be planted between roses or used as ground cover: dwarf juniper, dwarf spruce, dwarf pine, or the dwarfed wild form of the hemlock fir *(Tsuga mertensiana).*

Deciduous Shrubs

These also add variety to a planting of roses. Blooming at the same time with roses are:

• Alternate-leaf Butterfly Bush *(Buddleia alternifolia)*, lilac lavender-pink, June, 78–156 in. (200–300 cm) high; needs occasional rejuvenating pruning back to old wood.

• Old Man's Beard *(Chionanthus virginicus)*, creamy white, June, 117–156 in. (300–400 cm) high, very decorative with red and yellow roses; should not be combined with pink roses.

• Kousa Dogwood *(Cornus kousa)*, yellow greenish white, June, 195 in. (500 cm) high; red, edible fruit.

• Smokebush *(Cotinus coggygria)*, yellowish, reddish fruit stems, July to August, 78–117 in. (200–300 cm) high; broadly spreading, beautiful fall color.

• St.-John's-Wort *(Hypericum* species), yellow, July to October, $23^1/_2$–39 in. (60–100 m) high; the intense yellow goes with dark red and orange roses.

• Beautybush *(Kolkwitzia amabilis)*, light pink, May to June, 78–117 in. (200–300 cm) high; very beautiful with early white and red roses.

• Shrubby Cinquefoil *(Potentilla fruticosa)*, yellow, May to August, 39 in. (100 cm) high; with small yellow, rose-like flowers.

• Tamarisk *(Tamarix chinensis = T. pentandra)*, pinkish purple, July to August, 117–156 in (300–400 cm) high; shouldn't be combined with red and yellow roses.

• Common Boxwood *(Buxus sempervirens L.)* serves as a small box hedge for enclosed rose beds; pruned into hemispheres and pyramids and used as unpruned shrubs, it can be planted in sun or semi-shade as a focal point or a background.

Dwarf and Subshrubs

Some dwarf shrubs and subshrubs are among the most attractive companions for roses. Many are gray- to silvery-leaved, and their leaves have a spicy, aromatic scent—welcome characteristics in a rose neighborhood. Their culture is simple, needing much sun and an annual pruning.

• Blue Spirea *(Caryopteris incana)*, dark blue, September, 31 in. (80 cm) high.

• English Lavender *(Lavandula angustifolia Mill.)*, lavender blue, June to July, $19^1/_2$ in. (50 cm) high; goes with just about all rose colors; may only be cut back in spring, never into the old wood but only to at least one bunch of green leaves. This will inhibit fast aging.

• Perovskia *(Perovskia abrotanoides Karel)*, bluish, August to September, 47 in. (120 cm) high.

• Common Sage *(Salvia officinalis)*, lavender, June to July, $19^1/_2$ in. (50 cm) high; also in a red-leaved form.

Climbing Plants

Clematis species with their light to dark blue and white varieties offer themselves as partners to climbing roses. They are also very beautiful for walls or trellises behind higher shrub roses. Charming: *Clematis viticella* and its hybrids with many blue, bell-shaped flowers in July and August.

My tip: When choosing plants, be careful that the strong growth habit of a wild clematis—*Clematis vitalba*, for instance—does not endanger the rose.

Designing with ROSES

Grasses "Punctuate"

Grasses are always very clear, expressive characters, whose quality lies in the unequivocal linearity of their structure and outlines. They can be exclamation points, question marks, or dashes. And many bring a lighthearted playfulness into a planting. They can be used well among wild roses, but also in combination with floribundas and shrub roses.

My tip: Take up clumps every four years and divide.

Low Grasses
They are useful as boundary markers, as edging, or as a planting between groups of low bedding roses.

• The blue mounds of Blue Fescue *(Festuca cinerea)* and Valais Fescue *(Festuca valesiaca)* go very well with roses. Sheep's Fescue *(Festuca amethystina)* bears very beautiful purple spikelets, 12 in. (30 cm) high. Its coloring after flowering makes it interesting.

• You can also experiment with bluegrass species *(Sesleria)* and Woodrush *(Luzula nivea)*. The latter has outstanding silvery white, compact spikelets.

Taller Grasses
These become even more attractive toward fall because then they turn beautiful colors. The less the roses bloom toward fall, the more significant the grasses become. Therefore

you need to be aware that a yellow or brown fall color does not go equally well with all colors of roses. Silvery tones, on the other hand, are more compatible. Grasses can be planted singly or in groups.

• Feather reed grass *(Calamagrostis x acutiflora* "Karl Foerster") grows 70 in. (180 cm) high and is yellowish. Its effect is austere when, before and after flowering, the spikelets are leaning against the stem, and looser when the spikelets open during blooming or after the seeds have ripened.

• Eulalia *(Miscanthus sinensis),* with its monumental tufts, is used for structural framing in gardens and parks. Besides the many silver varieties, "Gracillimus" has a beautiful bronze tone in winter.

• Moor grass *(Molinia caerulea)* comes from the boglands and tolerates lime badly. Its subspecies *arundinacea* belongs to the garden varieties but is also found on mineral soils. Above the leaf crown ($19^1/_2$ in. [50 cm] high) rise the usually erect panicles (although they later loosen), which grow up to 78 in. (200 cm) high and are yellow in color. Recommended are "Karl Foerster," "Windspiel," and "Transparent."

• Indian grass *(Sorghastrum avenaceum)* is suitable for sunny, alkaline soil—$58^1/_2$ in. (150 cm) high, beautiful red fall color.

• Switchgrass *(Panicum virgatum)* is primarily known

through its variety "Rehbraun" (fawn colored), 47 in. (120 cm) high. The brown red summer color is very attractive between yellow roses, but it gets greener in seedlings

• Blue oat grass *(Helictorichon sempervirens)* is a suitable evergreen grass for small and medium-sized gardens in dry locations; it reaches a height of 47 in. (120 cm) with blue green tufts, which in June/July bloom with dependent panicles. The discoloring stems drop on their own.

• Atlas fescue *(Festuca mairei)* bears a few branched, slender panicles on 47-in. (120-cm) long, stiff stems. This beautiful green tufted grass is already blooming in June/July.

• Tufted hair grass *(Deschampsia cespitosa)* is a robust evergreen grass, up to 51 in. (130 cm) high, with drooping, rough leaves. The ample panicles bloom from July to August. Valuable varieties are "Bronzeschleier," "Goldschleier," and the late-blooming "Tautträger." Tufted hair grass loves damp soil or light semishade.

• Silver spikelet grass *(Achnatherum calamagrostis)* blooms from June to September with drooping panicles on stiff stems, becoming brownish after flowering.

• The genus of Needlegrasses *(Stipa)* has a long line of various tall species and subspecies, among which *Stipa barbata* is the most elegant. For it to develop in windy places, it should be planted loosely at intervals. The lime-loving native plant needs sun and grows to 27 in. (70 cm).

• Chinese Pennisetum *(Pennisetum alopecuroides)* forms decorative green tufts, which from the beginning of September are filled with fluffy, brownish pink, shimmering panicled ears. "Hameln" remains the best variety, being somewhat more compact than the species.

Shrub rose, magnificently grouped between shrubs and perennials. The *Moschata* hybrid "Penelope" together with the striking mullein "Gainsborough" and *Artemisia* "Lambrook Silver."

Annual Grasses
There are also grass species that bloom only once.

• Big Quaking Grass *(Briza maxima)* blooms from June to August and grows to a height of $15^{1}/_{2}$ in. (40 cm).

• Teff Love Grass *(Eragrostis tef)* is dainty at 27 in. (70 cm).

• Broomcorn, Millet *(Panicum miliaceum)* forms moplike panicles 39 in. (100 cm) in height.

Designing with ROSES

Annuals
(Summer Flowers)

Only a very few of the summer flowers, or annuals, coordinate well with roses, because their bright, lively colors—primarily yellows and reds—often overwhelm the roses.

Seeding outdoors: Only a few species, such as cornflowers (*Centaurea cyanus*), can be sown directly into the bed.

Starting seed under glass: Most annuals come into bloom earlier if you sow them in a small greenhouse or cold frame. Included among these is mealy-cup (*Salvia farinacea*),

Bedding roses in company. The heavy-blooming "Bonica '82" between the violet candles of *Veronica longifolia* "Blauriesin" and the globe-shaped flowers of the double poppy, *Papaver somniferum*.

by far one of the most beautiful annuals in combination with roses. It blooms purplish blue or silvery white from the end of June to the first heavy frost and is an invaluable space filler, 27 in. (70 cm) in height.

• Love-in-a-mist (*Nigella damascena*) bears a blue or white star-flower between the green filigree of the sepals. The delicate leaves make a striking contrast to the rose foliage.

• Sweet alyssum (*Lobularia maritima* var. *benthamii*) blooms as a low ground cover of 4 to 8 in. (10 to 20 cm) in height from June to October in the colors of lavender, purple, blue violet, rose red, and white. Beginning in May it can be sown where it is to grow. Just press the seed in, and don't cover it. It should sprout after 10 days. Alyssum is recommended as an undercover for standards because you needn't bother about it when laying down the crown in early winter.

• Candytuft (*Iberis amara* [rocket]: white; *Iberis umbellata* [globe candytuft]: white, violet, purple) bears walnut-shaped inflorescences from June to August and grows to 10 in. (25 cm). Seed from March to May. Cutting back the faded flowers promotes renewed flowering.

• A magnificent sage species is gentian sage (*Salvia patens*), whose flowers 2 in. (6 cm) across occur alone or in bunches of several on a stem. The distinctive intense ultramarine blue labiate flowers drop quickly but work especially well with dark red roses. Instead of taking up the corms in fall like dahlias to overwinter, it's advisable to sow again in February under glass.

• *Salvia horminum* (= *viridis*), 23 in. (60 cm) tall, is decorative, with blue violet, pale pink, or white bracts, depending on the variety.

• Of the verbenas, the following go with roses: *Verbena rigida* (vervain), lilac blue, 12 in. (30 cm) tall; *Verbena canadensis* (rose verbena), violet purple, 16 in. (40 cm) tall; *Verbena bonariensis*, lilac blue, 47 in. (120 cm) tall.

• Among the flowers of high summer are two in the mallow family with a good effect from a distance: tree mallow (*Lavatera trimestris*), pink, white, and *Malope trifida*, red, purple, pink, white, both June to October, 31–35 in. (80–90 cm) tall.

• The blue throatwort (*Trachelium caeruleum*) bears tiny little blue violet or white flowers in flat corymbs from July to September. It thrives in sunny and semishady places and grows to 27 in. (70 cm).

Biennials

Neither perennial nor annual, and yet invaluable for rose gardens, are the biennials. Some sow themselves in the garden. However, you should avoid transplanting them if posssible.

• Common foxglove (*Digitalis purpurea*) permits exciting color combinations. It grows to a height of 78 in. (200 cm).

Caution: Poisonous plant!

• The mulleins (*Verbascum* species) love sun and dryness, but they also thrive in any well-drained garden soil. Most beautiful species: *Verbascum leianthum*, very tall and vigorously branching; *Verbascum longifolium*, 47 in. (120 cm) tall and white with hairs (tomen-tose); *Verbascum olympicum*, whitely tomentose, candelabralike, $58^{1}/_{2}$ in. (150 cm) tall with large yellow flowers.

• Honesty, or money plant (*Lunaria annua*) has almost circular fruit with a silvery septum. It blooms lavender purple, grows 47 in. (120 cm) tall, and seeds itself.

• The silver sage (*Salvia argentea*) is one of the especially beautiful sage species, yet it is still not widely known. These are really shrubs, but they die back after blooming and are therefore better described as "biennial." This sage develops large, silver-sided, hairy, oval leaves in rosettes. The inflorescence is branched, 23 in. (60 cm) high, and in June and July bears white flowers with yellow lips.

• Clary (*Salvia sclarea*) grows similarly, but in June and July of the second year it bears an abundantly branching inflorescence with light lavender flowers above pinky red subtending leaves. It thrives outstandingly in dry, warm situations and seeds itself.

• The Scotch thistle (*Onopordum bracteatum*) is a decorative member of the Composite family with silver gray foliage. Leaves strewn with thorns, the stalk (over 78 in. [200 cm] tall) and the reddish thistle flowers ornament this eye-catcher. The plants work best as single plants in the natural garden with shrub roses. They sow themselves.

Designing with ROSES

Roses and Perennials

The possibilities for creating a garden using perennials and roses are inexhaustible. Because of their differing nutrient requirements, however, don't mix roses and perennials; plant them in bands or set them at right angles to each other. That way you can target the fertilizing.

The following companion perennials were chosen not only for color but also for structural characteristics (see table on pages 78 and 79).

Ground-covering perennials: Perennials that have a central root and just spread on the soil aboveground are relatively harmless to roses, for they only "mulch" the soil.

• For dwarf roses, the large-flowered winter savory (*Satureja montana* "Coerulea"), which produces light blue flowers in August and scarcely roots its low-lying shoots, is a recommended companion.

• The following are classified as conditionally threatening for roses: myrtle (*Vinca*), false miterwort (*Tiarella*), waldsteinia (*Waldsteinia*), dead nettle (*Lamium*), lungwort (*Pulmonaria*), self-heal (*Prunella*), betony (*Stachys*), some cranesbills (*Geranium*), thyme (*Thymus*), soapwort (*Saponaria*), and epimedium (*Epimedium*). At most they can be considered for edging.

• Never plant either acaena (*Acaena buchanii*) or plumbago

(*Ceratostigma plumbaginoides*) between roses. The root systems of these plants will strangle the roses.

Veil-like and cloud-like flowers are delicate and unassuming and thus also provide very good background for roses.

• Lady's-mantle (*Alchemilla mollis*) provides wonderful contrast for red roses. On the other hand, its own color accentuates white roses, and for yellow varieties it creates tone-on-tone nuances.

• Baby's-breath (*Gypsophila paniculata*) suggests weightlessness. It thus needs a strong color next to it.

• The light lavender calamint (*Calamintha nepeta*) blooms from July to frost and provides food for bees.

• Marjoram (*Origanum vulgare*) can be planted with all roses with the exception of orange reds. Its blooming season (July to September) can be lengthened by cutting back.

• The indian-physic (*Gillenia trifoliata*) thrives outstandingly in light semishade behind and between shrub roses.

• For the fall bloomers the clouds of flowers of hardy asters are suitable (*Aster ericoides* [heath aster], *Aster cordifolius* [bluewood aster], *Aster laevis*, *Aster vimineus*, *Aster lateriflorus*.

Candles of all sizes: By candle flowers we mean slender, vertical inflorescences. The stronger the color contrast, the smaller the number there should be in the planting.

Completely in its element—the ground-cover rose "Immensee." Next to it on the left the flower-candles of *Acanthus* and *Salvia sclarea*.

Important: Almost all delphinium varieties bloom a second time in September if the plants are cut back to the ground immediately after blooming.

Caution: Aconite and delphinium are poisonous plants. Avoid touching the leaves and

Globe-shaped flowers draw the eye because of their striking form, but their colors are almost never dominating. They must be placed carefully. Beautiful spheres of flowers at rose time are produced by the various decorative *allium* species and globe thistles.

Trumpet-shaped flowers are highly expressive flower forms. Therefore you could use lilies as special focal points. In colors of white and purple, but also in yellows, they are noble companions for roses. Mallows bloom in the poorer rose months.

Loose panicles and clusters: In this group there are only a few eye-catchers like the plume poppy or phlox. Most of these plants do not have a particularly rigid flower form and do not get so tall that they become focal points. Many could also be considered for ground covers or medium-tall in-between plantings for roses.

Stars and disks:

• Rough-leaved asters (*Aster novae-angliae*) and smooth-leaved asters (*Aster novae-belgii*) are good rose companions in fall.

• With their extremely precise stars, the eryngos (*Eryngium* species) form a very impressive, almost bizarre contrast for roses.

Tiered flowers are rare, but phlomis (*Phlomis russeliana*), in light yellow and silver, is uniquely beautiful with yellow roses.

wear gloves (see also Important Notice, page 159)

Bell-shaped flowers:

• The bellflowers (*Campanula* species) with their various shades of blue or blue-favoring shades of violet to rose to white are important rose companions. The low-lying kinds can be used as edging plants, while the medium and tall species can be planted in between; the latter also may be used for background shrubs, because they are taller than most bedding roses. Their bright green leaves, which form a nice contrast with the rose foliage, are another reason for planting them.

• "Schellenbaum" is the name of a decorative variety of the needle palm (*Yucca filamentosa*). With its light yellow or creamy white color, it does very well alone between yellow or vivid red roses. An eye-catcher, but only for fully sunny locations.

Designing with ROSES

Name	Color of variety	Blooming season	Height in in. (cm)	Location and Notes
1. Veil-like and Cloud-like Flowers				
Lady's-mantle *Alchemilla mollis*	green yellow	June–Aug.	12–20 (30–50)	full sun to semishade; damp
Calaminth *Calamintha nepeta*	white, pale lavender	July–Sept.	12–31 (30–80)	sunny; porous soil; spicy leaves
Colewort *Crambe cordifolia*	white	June–July	55–78 (140–200)	full sun, warm; not too dry; large leaves
Indian-physic *Gillenia trifoliata*	white with reddish calyx	June–July	40 (100)	sunny to semishade; soil not too heavy
Baby's-breath *Gypsophila paniculata*	white	June–Aug.	31–47 (80–120)	full sun; porous soil
Statice *Limonum latifolium*	light violet dark blue	May–July	20–31 (50–80)	full sun; porous soil
2. Candles of All Sizes				
Garden aconite *Aconitum napellus,* and others	dark blue, white	June–July	35–59 (90–150)	semishade, cool, humid
Bugbane *Cimicifuga simplex,* and others	white, creamy white	Sept.–Oct.	40–55 (100–140)	semishade to shady; for the background
Delphinium *Delphinium-Belladonna*-hybrids	white, light and azure blue, dark violet	June–July Aug.–Sept.	31–47 (80–120)	sunny to partially sunny, cool; rich soil
Desert-candle *Eremurus* species	white, yellow	June–July	59–98 (150–250)	sunny; porous soil, high fertility
Gay-feather *Liatris spicata*	violet pink, violet, white	July–Sept.	16–35 (40–90)	sunny; porous soil, high fertility
Speedwell *Veronica longifolia*	medium blue, deep blue, white	July–Aug.	20–47 (50–120)	sunny, warm; soil fertile, loamy
3. Bell-shaped Flowers				
Giant bellflower *Campanula lactiflora*	milky blue, white, lavender pink	June–July	20–59 (50–150)	light shade, cool; fertile soil
Wood bellflower *Campanula latifolia*	blue violet, white	June–July	31–40 (80–100)	light to part shade; damp
Clustered bellflower *Campanula glomerata*	dark violet, pure white	June–Aug.	6–23 (15–60)	sunny, warm; no sogginess
Balloon flower *Platycodon grandiflorus*	medium blue, white, pink, violet blue	July–Aug.	8–27 (20–70)	sunny; soil porous, rich in nutrients
4. Globular Flowers				
Alliums, Chives *Allium* species	purple violet, lavender, pink	May–Aug.	12–40 (30–100)	sunny; good soil, moderately dry, porous
Globe thistle *Echinops* species	blue	July–Sept.	31–47 (80–120)	sunny, warm, protected from wind; porous soil
Sheep's bit *Jasione laevis*	blue lavender	July–Aug.	8–16 (20–40)	full sun; lime-poor soil, not too heavy

Name	Color of variety	Blooming season	Height in in. (cm)	Location and Notes
5. Trumpet Flowers				
Hollyhock *Alcea rosea*	pink, purple, red, white, yellow	June–Sept.	35–78 (90–200)	sunny; rich, loose soil
Tree mallow *Lavatera thuringiaca*	light pink	July–Sept.	59 (150)	semishade
Madonna lily *Lilium candidum*	white	June–July	31–47 (80–120)	sunny, warm, protected; rich soil
Royal lily *Lilium regale*	white inside, brownish pink outside	July	23–59 (60–150)	sunny; root region shaded; rich soil
Musk mallow, etc. *Malva moschata,* etc.	pink, white	June–Sept.	16–31 (40–80)	sunny; ground not too damp; self-seeds easily
Sidalcea *Sidalcea* hybrids	pink, red, purple red, white	June–Sept.	23–40 (60–100)	full sun; lime-poor, porous soil
6. Loose Panicles and Clusters				
Dittany *Dictamnus albus*	white, pink	May–July	23–40 (60–100)	sunny to semishady, warm
Plume poppy *Macleaya cordata*	white	July–Aug.	78–117 (200–300)	soil light, warm
Perennial phlox *Phlox paniculata* hybrids	light pink, violet, white, red, orange	June–Sept.	23–31 (60–80)	full sun, high humidity; rich soil
Sage/salvia *Salvia nemorosa*	violet blue, medium blue	May–Aug.	16–31 (40–80)	sunny, warm; soil porous, rich
Common sage *Salvia officinalis*	violet blue	June–July	12–23 (30–60)	sunny, warm; dry, porous, chalky soil
Skullcap *Scutellaria incana,* and others	bluish white	July–Oct.	16–23 (40–60)	semishade, warm
7. Stars and Disks				
Yarrow *Achillea* hybrids	pink, orange, crimson red	June–Aug.	12–31 (30–80)	full sun, warm; for all garden soils
Japanese anemone *Anemone japonica* hybrids	pink, white	Aug.–Oct.	31–55 (80–140)	semishade; moderately rich soil
Oxeye *Buphthalmum salicifolium*	golden yellow	June–Sept.	12–23 (30–60)	sunny; chalky soil
Tickseed *Coreopsis grandiflora*	yellow	June–Sept.	23–35 (60–90)	sunny, warm; soil moderately rich
Tickseed *Coreopsis verticillata*	golden yellow	June–Sept.	12–27 (30–70)	sunny; soil moderately rich; no sandy soil
Eryngo *Eryngium planum, E. alpinum*	deep blue, silvery violet	June–July	20–35 (50–90)	sunny, warm; dry, porous soil
Cranesbill *Geranium sanguineum*	crimson red, white	May–Aug.	4–20 (10–50)	sunny to semishade; dry soil
Perennial flax *Linum perenne,* and others	blue, light blue	May–July	12–20 (30–50)	full sun, warm; porous soil
Bouncing Bet *Saponaria officinalis*	pink, white	June–Sept.	23–31 (60–80)	full sun; porous soil

Designing with ROSES

Rose Luxuries

Many roses possess the wonderful characteristic of magnificent scent. In the Orient, rosewater and rose oil (attar of roses) were popular as cosmetics and massaging oil. The Romans bathed in water with rose petals. In the Middle Ages, the rose served as a medicine for all sorts of complaints.

The costly attar of roses is obtained through distillation, enfleurage, pressing, and extraction. Europe's chief areas of cultivation are in Bulgaria and France. The Damask rose (*Rosa damascena* "Trigintipetala") is cultivated in the valley of Kazanlik in Bulgaria. The centifolia rose (*Rosa centifolia*, the hundred-petaled rose) blooms in the region of Grasse in the South of France. At least 6614 lb (3000 kg) of flowers are needed to get 2 lb 3 oz (1 kg) of rose oil. Rose flowers are also used in the production of soap, perfume, potpourris, and palate pleasers like jam and punch. If you'd like to try making them yourself, you'll find some suggestions below—all for use only with roses that haven't been sprayed, of course!

Rose Punch

This refreshing drink is the crowning glory at any party. For eight people you need $10^{1}/_{2}$ to 14 oz (300 to 400 g) of fragrant rose petals, which you sprinkle with $5^{1}/_{4}$ oz (150 g) of sugar and drizzle with 2 tsp

(10 mL) of orange liqueur. Let the mixture stand for one hour covered in the refrigerator. Then pour 1 qt (1 L) of dry white wine over it and again chill for one hour. Strain and then shortly before serving add a bottle of ice-cold champagne. Float fresh rose petals on the punch for decoration.

Rose Tea

Steep a handful of dried rose petals in $12^{1}/_{2}$ oz ($^{3}/_{4}$ L) of water and let stand for 10 minutes. Drink hot, sweetened with honey, or cold, flavored with lemon. Rose tea [it is sometimes claimed] calms the heart and strengthens the liver and gallbladder.

Rose Jam

You need fresh rose petals of 20 double roses, 2 lb 3oz (1 kg) of "jelly sugar" (i.e., sugar with pectin), 1 qt (1 L) of water, and the juice of 4 lemons. Put the rose petals in the water, add the lemon juice and jelly sugar, and stir well. Allow the whole thing to boil for half an hour. Place in jars.

Rose Hips for the Table

The fruits of the rose, which are very rich in vitamins, can also be made into tea, marmalade, paste, and wine and are extremely healthful—so long as they haven't come into contact with chemical sprays.

Rose Potpourri

Take $3^{1}/_{2}$ oz (100 g) of rose petals, 1 oz (30 g) of flowers of

the Roman camellia, 1 oz (30 g) of orange peel, 1 oz (30 g) of lavender flowers, 1 cinnamon stick (finely ground), and 10 drops of rose oil. Mix ingredients together, put in a screw-top jar, and keep jar tightly closed for two weeks. Then place your potpourri in a pretty bowl. To refresh its pleasant scent, add a few drops of rose oil.

The charm of the unusual—
"Landora," ordinarily a yellow
hybrid tea, can appear overcast with
pink after cold nights in the fall.
Similar color change has also been
observed in "Gloria Dei" and
"Schneewittchen."

A basket of roses,
a basket of fragrance.

Rose
PORTRAITS
The Most Beautiful and the Hardiest Species and Varieties

Should they bloom simply and gracefully, classically or lushly in your garden? With their pale pastel colors or strong hues and their intoxicating fragrances, roses cast a spell over every garden, large or small. The choice is yours!

"Mme Isaac Pereire," a very fragrant Hybrid Perpetual rose, blooms several times, producing intensely colored flowers. Here they are adorned with violet cranesbill, *Geranium ibericum.*

Roses in PORTRAITS

The Most Beautiful and the Healthiest Roses

In the following plant portraits you'll get to know the most popular and the best roses for the large and small garden—among them the most important roses in the world—some special recommendations by the author, and also some hybrids from the former East Germany. The selection offered reflects the full range of the rose's variety, in order to meet every design need.

What You Will Find

In order to make the selections descriptive and visible at a glance, the roses are divided into distinct groups, which are similar to the often varying groupings in the different rose catalogs.

The author's best recommendations are presented to you in pictures and text. This selection is necessarily condensed. You will find more varieties—often no less worth mentioning—in the tables at the ends of each section and the most important attributes of each rose listed there.

Wild roses and their hybrids— *see pages 86 to 93.* It is advisable to make a distinction within this group between the European species and the non-European ones because the former are often adapted to a different climatic zone.

Climbing roses—*see pages 94 to 103.* The growth type determines the arrangement of this section, for climbing roses can be divided into the soft-caned—usually small-flowered ramblers, and the stiff-caned—usually somewhat larger-flowered climbers; they also have accordingly different uses in the garden. Both groups include once-blooming and repeat-blooming varieties.

Shrub roses—*see pages 104 to 123.* This large group is divided into modern varieties, old roses, and English roses. There are once-blooming and repeat-blooming varieties in each subdivision.

Ground covers—*see pages 124 to 131.* Here you will find roses that cover the ground thickly and thus allow few weeds to come up. Among these are low-growing, creeping varieties but also bush-height hybrids. Many rose novices are thus confused when they see a rose offered in one catalog as a shrub rose and in another as a ground-cover rose. These taller ground-cover roses are also called embankment roses and are shrub roses that are also suitable for use as ground covers.

Bedding roses—*see pages 132 to 149.* The International Union of Rose Societies of the World has made the suggestion that bedding roses be divided into "large-flowered" and "cluster-flowered" roses according to their blooms because these criteria are immediately understandable to everyone. The large-flowered roses include the hybrid teas; the cluster-flowered ones include the floribundas, the polyanthas, and their hybrids; even the miniature roses are ranked there, although they are treated separately internationally. Classification problems arise with varieties that are both large-flowered and cluster-flowered. Here the character of the rose in question must be the decisive factor. Thus in the text the old designations "hybrid tea" and "floribunda" always continue to be used in historical contexts, because at that time the new terminology did not exist.

Cascades and standards—*see pages 150 to 153.* In this group you will find varieties that can be grafted onto standards successfully. Not every rose is optimally suitable for this. If rambler roses are grafted onto a standard, we then speak of cascade roses; earlier they were called hanging or weeping roses. All the others are so-called standards. The varieties named here can also of course be used without a standard in their own groupings—grafted at the neck of the root.

Structure of the Rose Portraits

All the rose portraits are structured to be clear and concise.

The name of the rose appears in boldface over the description. Depending on the rose, this can be either the botanical species name or the variety name. With some wild roses you will find after this name the shortened name, in regular type, of the first person to describe the species. Some roses have different names in other countries. Then the synonym is given in parentheses.

Earlier classification, grower, and first commercial introduction are given as appropriate under the name. Here it is also mentioned if and when a variety has received the ADR label (see page 44) or has been chosen a "world rose."

The description is arranged by the following headings: Buds, Flowers, Growth, Foliage, and Use. Additional information about health, fragrance, thorns, frost hardiness, and so forth will be found under the final heading, "My tip."

Specifications and Their Accuracy

All figures should be understood as median values; great variations can occur in individual cases, such as in location or cultivation.

• The flower diameter is aways indicated by the symbol Ø.

• The figure for height of growth is based on the average height of the plant in the second year, but with climbing roses in the fourth year. Since the height of growth depends very much on the quality of the soil, great differences can occur here.

Alba rose "Great Maiden's Blush" with attractive companions like "Veilchenblau" (behind), with variegated dogwood (left rear), and red cranesbill, *Geranium psilostemon* (left front).

The color descriptions are subjective attempts to describe the standard of a particular rose, but they can also vary for a number of reasons.

The fragrance descriptions attempt to give an impression of the scent of a plant. Intensity, perception, and judgment of a scent are, however, dependent on the location of the rose, the time of day, and the weather, as well as on the sense of the beholder.

WILD ROSES

Without wild roses there would be no roses! They are the first ancestors of all varieties, they grow as shrubs, they can climb and creep—but almost all of them bloom only once a year. In fall, on the other hand, they cover themselves with magnificent rose hips.

Wild roses are very fashionable now, for more and more people are yearning to "get back to nature" in their garden. Is it the simple, single flowers, is it the delicacy, form, and exuberant color of the five-petaled flowers and their for-the-most-part magnificent stamens that charm us, or the diverse hips, or even the fierce, prominent thorns? With more than a thousand-year-old adaptation to their location, each wild-rose species has maintained its own harmonious individuality. Moreover, the diversity of nature has an ecological significance if you consider that wild roses provide the basic requirements of life for many animals.

Dealing with Wild Roses

Wild roses grow on their own roots, so they may be sold as propagated by seed or cuttings or grafted to an "alien" stock. But the growth of a grafted scion may be influenced and changed by the other, truly alien vigor of the root stock. Therefore you should only plant wild roses grown on their own roots.

• Rose lovers and environmentalists do well to advocate the preservation of native wild roses in their natural locations. In the open countryside it would be preferable to plant seedlings with their rich genetic potential for variety. Unfortunately such plants are hardly ever seen on the market because of cost considerations.

• For the garden it's advisable to buy from a grower a plant produced from a cutting of a wild rose species with the flowers and size desired.

• Selected as stocks for grafting, often the thornless wild rose types are unsuitable for natural plantings.

Origins Are Important

In the following portraits both European and non-European wild roses are presented.

European wild roses are by nature entirely winter hardy and adapt well to our soil and climate conditions—provided you choose the location according to their requirements. They need neither water nor pesticides, which some species won't even tolerate.

With the non-European wild roses there are differences in winter hardiness and in their culture requirements. Their hips are often well received by the birds.

The hybrids that often occur among wild rose species, which can be very beautiful, are difficult to categorize. The hybrid below probably has contributions from *Rosa pimpinellifolia*, possibly also *Rosa tomentosa* and *Rosa pendulina*. In the picture to the right: the native *Rosa coriifolia*.

WILD ROSES

Rosa pendulina L.

(= *Rosa alpina* L.)
Alpine hedge rose.
Native to: Mountains of south and central Europe. Relative of the *Rosa moyesii* from China.
Buds pointed oval. Flowers brilliant rose red to purple red with light centers and striking yellow stamens, 2 in. (5 cm) Ø, single, blooming from end of May to June. Hips long oval, vase-shaped, dark red, retained into winter. Growth upright to overhanging. In garden 59 in. (150 cm) tall. Frequently runners. Canes red brown, thin, without thorns near flowers. Foliage soft with 7–9 leaflets. Use for hedges and fences.

My tip: Good combined with climbing plants like *Clematis alpina* or other loose bushes.

Rosa pimpinellifolia L.

Scotch rose, Burnet rose.
Native to: On the dunes of the North Sea islands it creates a carpet of roses up to 8 in. (20 cm) high. In the central mountains of Scotland it grows up to 39 in. (100 cm) tall. Buds rounded, small, light yellow. Flowers cream-colored, rarely light yellow. Medium size, 2 in. (5 cm) Ø, disk-shaped with 5 petals, numerous, but only one to a short cane; fine wild rose scent; very early-blooming (middle of May). Hips deep purple-black or brown-black, glossy at first; smooth, flattened sphere, only medium-sized; begin to color as early as July and are not taken by the birds. Growth very delicate-caned, brushy, thickly thorned, upright in garden, twiggy, up to 47 in. (120 cm) tall. Sends out runners. Foliage very delicate, 7–9 round, often gray green leaflets, which become red in fall.

Rosa pendulina

Rosa pimpinellifolioa var. *altaica*

Rosa glauca

Rosa rubinigosa

Use for cover plantings and protection, for hedges, bushes, slopes. Thrives on its own roots in the poorest soils.

My tip: To avoid early aging, cut back radically every 6–7 years to 4 in. (10 cm) above the ground.

Rosa glauca Pourr.

(= *Rosa rubrifolia* Vill.)
Native to: European mountains.
Buds small, numerous, usually single. Flowers crimson pink, 1–1½ in. (3–4 cm) Ø, unevenly radially symmetrical, once-blooming. Hips round, ½ in. (1.5 cm) Ø, red with protruding calyx. Growth upright, slightly overhanging, finely branching, up to 98 in. (250 cm) high. Branches brown red; few straight or hooklike thorns. Foliage loose, brown red to bluish, furnished with 5–7 leaflets, not hairy. Use for cover and for full shrubs for mixed hedges, embankments. Charming in groups but also as single plants. Undemanding.

Central European Species

Rosa canina

Rosa gallica

My tip: Susceptible to rust. As it ages, cut back to 4 in. (10 cm) above the ground, except for one-year-old supporting canes. Grows even in semishade but blooms less there.

Rosa canina L.
Dog rose.
Native to: Europe. Edges of fields.
Buds oval, pointed, pink. Flowers pale pink to white; medium-sized, $1\frac{1}{2}$ to 2 in. (4–5 cm) Ø, saucer of 5 petals with dense yellow stamens, usually short-stemmed, alone or several in a cluster. True wild rose fragrance. Blooming season June as a rule, brief but very beautiful. Hips orange to scarlet red, long oval, $\frac{3}{4}$ in. (2 cm), smooth and shining; often become soft only after prolonged frost and then picked at by birds. Growth upright, usually umbrellalike, also overhanging, more than 117 in. (300 cm) high, climbing by means of hooked thorns. Foliage green with

blue-green shimmer, 5–7 leaflets, hairless. Use as individual, in groups—also with other shrubs. Good bird-sheltering shrub, no care. Related species: **Rosa rubiginosa** L. (= *Rosa eglanteria* L.) Eglantine or sweetbriar rose; in growth very similar, but not so tall, denser and sturdier thorns; flowers smaller and more intense pink; scent of the foliage like fresh apples, as also many of its hybrids.
My tip: Somewhat susceptible to cicadas and spider mites, but almost no fungus. Never prune—only for rejuvenation with age, cut back to 4 in. (10 cm) above the ground.

Rosa gallica L.
French rose.
Native to: southern and central Europe, also Asia Minor. Vineyards.
Buds pointed globular, pink. Flowers pink to bright red, lighter at the center; large, $2\frac{3}{4}$–3 in. (7–8 cm) Ø, 5 delicate petals, fragrant. Usually grow one to a stem. Bloom beginning of June to July. Hips round, tile-red. Growth with thin canes up to $19\frac{1}{2}$ in. (50 cm) long; underground runners, which usually creep a great distance. Thorns needlelike, numerous. Foliage large, coarse. Use as small shrub or ground cover on dry ground, also in semishade. Also recommended: From this species comes the Apothecary Rose, *Rosa gallica* "Officinalis" (see page 110).
My tip: Susceptible to mildew. Much light, but better with semishade at midday, since the petals burn easily.

WILD ROSES

Rosa moyesii Hemsl. & Wils.
Native to: western China.
The most beautiful garden form will be described below. The wild species is larger, its flowers usually somewhat brighter.
"Geranium" Wisley Gardens, 1945
<u>Buds</u> roundish, red. <u>Flowers</u> dark scarlet; medium-sized, 2 in. (6 cm) Ø, single, shallow, saucer flower, 5 broad petals; striking yellow stamens; greenish yellow stigma disk; flowers alone or several on one cane, scentless. <u>Hips</u> bottle-shaped, large; 3 in. (8 cm) long, orange at first, then brilliant red, with scattered bristles and beautiful sepals. <u>Growth</u> more contained than the wild variety, 78–117 in. (200–300 cm) tall. Yellowish thorns, arranged almost in pairs. <u>Foliage</u> medium green, glossy, with 9–13 leaflets. <u>Use</u> in hedges or alone, 98 in. (250 cm) or more apart. <u>Also recommended:</u> "High-downensis," a sport of *Rosa moyesii*.
My tip: Never prune!

Rosa roxburghii Tratt.
Chestnut rose, Chinquapin rose.
Native to: Japan and China.
<u>Buds</u> medium-sized, pointed oval. <u>Flowers</u> white or palely light pink; 2 in. (6 cm) Ø, slightly fragrant; blooms beginning of June. <u>Hips</u> flattened globular, 1 in. (3 cm) Ø, very thorny, green even when ripe, soon drop. <u>Growth</u> upright, very branching; 97$\frac{1}{2}$ in. (250 cm) high and wide. Bark on two-year-old and older wood finely flaking, gray; thorns and leaf axils paired; frosthardy. <u>Foliage</u> unusually long, with 9–15 elliptical leaflets scarcely roselike. Beautiful yellow brown fall coloring. <u>Use</u> by itself. <u>Also recommended:</u> *Rosa x micrugosa*

Rosa moyesii "Geranium"

Henkel, with orange red hips, arose from a cross with *Rosa rugosa*.

Rosa wichuraiana Crép.
Native to: Japan, Korea, East China.
<u>Buds</u> small, round. <u>Flowers</u> white; 1$\frac{1}{2}$ in. (4 cm) Ø, several to a small panicle, slightly scented, not blooming until July. <u>Hips</u> small, oval. <u>Growth</u> vigorous, canes 117–195 in. (300–500 cm) long and very supple, thus often creeping, green with fat,

Non-European Species

Rosa roxburghii

Rosa wichuraiana

Rosa rugosa

Rosa nutkana

Rosa multiflora

Rosa nutkana Pall.
Native to: western North America, coastal regions of Alaska to northern California.
<u>Buds</u> medium-sized, pointed oval. <u>Flowers</u> lavender pink; rather large, 2 in. (6 cm) Ø, saucer-shaped, usually alone. <u>Hips</u> round, $^3/_4$ in. (2 cm) Ø, smooth, brilliant tile red, shining, translucent. <u>Growth</u> tight, upright, 78 in. (200 cm) tall, canes thin, dark brown, usually bristly. <u>Foliage</u> dark-green, hairy on the back, 5–9 leaflets. <u>Use</u> for untrimmed hedges. Space 59 in. (150 cm) apart. <u>Also recommended:</u> *Rosa yainacensis* and *Rosa nutkana* "Cantab," with larger flowers.

Rosa multiflora Thunb.
Many-flowered rose.
Native to: Japan and Korea.
<u>Buds</u> small, round. <u>Flowers</u> white; small, $^3/_4$ in. (2 cm) Ø, large clusters of many, fragrant. Blooms end of June. <u>Hips</u> pea-sized, slightly less than $^1/_4$ in. (0.5 cm) Ø, rounded oval, red, very much loved by birds. <u>Growth</u> strongly arching, overhanging, over 156 in (400 cm) high, climbing, soon densely branching, bushy; thornless to some degree. <u>Foliage</u> light green, usually with 9 leaflets. At the leaf axils are ciliated bracts. <u>Use</u> mostly as hedges. Large space requirements. Space 117 in. (300 cm) apart. <u>Also recommended:</u> *Rosa multiflora* "Carnea," whose double flowers are pale pink at first, later white.

hooked thorns. <u>Foliage</u> small, with 7–9 dark green, very shiny, oval leaflets. <u>Use</u> as semi-evergreen ground-cover rose; canes lying on the ground root very easily. <u>Also recommended:</u> "Grandiflora" has somewhat larger flowers and inflorescences. *Rosea luciae* Franch & Rochebr., with stiffer growth and fewer flowers.
  My tip: Needs well-drained soil to avoid damp roots.

Rosa rugosa Thunb.
Japanese rose.
Native to: northeastern Asia. Meanwhile also established in Europe.
<u>Buds</u> oval, pointed. <u>Flowers</u> old rose or rose red, also pure white; large, $3^1/_2$ in (9 cm) Ø, saucer-shaped, 5 petals, alone or in bunches on short, bristly stems; strong, very good fragrance. Blooms until mid-September, slowing down somewhat later. <u>Hips</u> very large, flattened globular, smooth, orange to tile red. <u>Growth</u> upright,

tight, very thickly branched, 70 in. (180 cm), tall, very frost-hardy; dense, bristly thorns. <u>Foliage</u> 5–7 wrinkled leaflets with prominent veins, dark green. <u>Use</u> in the city along streets, in gardens, not on the open landscape. Very popular because of its continuous flowering, uncommon for wild roses, and its fruits. Usable singly and in groups. Numerous varieties.
  My tip: Tolerates salt, but extremely sensitive to pH value over 6, when it inclines toward chlorosis. Allergic to fertilizers containing lime, otherwise very healthy. Inexpensive to care for. With age, cut back radically to 4 in. (10 cm) high.

WILD ROSES

Species and variety	Native to	Flower	Hip	Height in in. (cm)	Comments
European Wild Roses and Hybrids					
Rosa agrestis Savi.	S., W., central Europe, N. Africa	pale pink to white, 1 in. (3 cm) Ø	oval orange red	78 (200)	Field rose.
Rosa arvensis Huds.	central, S. Europe	white, ¾–1 in. (2–3 cm) Ø	oval, ¾ in. (2 cm) long, bright red	39–78 (100–200)	Field rose, thin canes, also loves to climb.
Rosa corifolia Fries. = *Rosa caesia*	central Europe, Asia Minor	pink, 1–1½ in. (3–4 cm) Ø	round, sepals	59 (150)	Var. *froebelii* = rose understock "Laxa."
Rosa corymbifera Borkh.	Europe to N. Africa, Asia Minor	white to light pink, 1–1½ in. (3–4 cm) Ø	oval, orange to scarlet	98–117 (250–300)	Similar to *Rosa canina* L. but leaflets hairy.
Rosa majalis Herrm.	Europe to Russia	crimson red 1½ in. (4 cm) Ø	round, nearly ½ in. (1 cm) Ø, sepals	59–78 (150–200)	May rose, cinnamon rose.
Rosa micrantha Sm.	central, S. Europe	pinky white, ¾–1 in. (2–3 cm) Ø	small, without sepals	39–70 (100–180)	Small-flowered rose, similar to *Rosa rubiginosa* L.
Rosa mollis Sm.	N., W. Europe	dark pink,1½–2 in. (4–5 cm) Ø	round, ripen early, sepals	39 (100)	Similar to *Rosa villosa* L., smaller.
Rosa rubiginosa L.	all Europe	light pink, 1–1½ in. (3–4 cm) Ø	oval, sepals	78–117 (200–300)	Eglantine, sweetbriar; thick thorns; good variety: "Magnifica."
Rosa scabriuscula Sm.	W.,E., central Europe	light pink, 1½ in. (4 cm) Ø	round, glandular-hispid, sepals	78–117 (200–300)	Scratchy rose, like *Rosa tomentosa* Sm., but with prickly canes and leaves.
Rosa sherardii Davies	Europe exc. eastern	dark pink, 1 in. (3 cm) Ø	circular sepals adhere a long time	78 (200)	Dense growth, short branches, leaflets hairy on top, felted underneath.
Rosa tomentosa Sm.	Europe to Caucasus	light pink/white, 1½ in. (4 cm) Ø	round, ½ in. (1.5 cm) Ø, red, with stem glands	78 (200)	Felted rose (because of the feltlike hairy leaves), velvet rose.
Rosa x macrantha Desp.	France	pale pink, soon pure white, 2¾ in. (7 cm) Ø	round, dull red, ½ in. (1.5 cm), bare	59 (150)	Hybrid. Outstanding beautiful stamens.
Rosa x reversa (= *Rosa rubella* Sm.)	Grower Waldstein & Kid 1820	pink, early, ½ in. (1.5 cm) Ø	oval, dark red	59 (150)	Hybrid. *R. pendulina x Rosa pimpinellifolia;* purple canes.
Rosa x ruga Lindl.	Bred in Italy before 1830	light pink, 2 in. (5 cm) Ø, loosely double, in large panicles	—	117 (300)	Hybrid. Descended from *Rosa arvensis*.

Species and variety	Native to	Flower	Hip	Height in in. (cm)	Comments

Non-European Wild Roses and Hybrids

Species and variety	Native to	Flower	Hip	Height in in. (cm)	Comments
Rosa ecae Aitchis.	Afghanistan, Turkestan	golden yellow, $^1/_2$–$^3/_4$ in. (1–2 cm) Ø	small, round	51 (130)	Leaves and flowers very like the *Potentilla.* Only variety "Golden Chersonese."
Rosa foetida Herrm.	Asia Minor, Afghanistan	intense yellow, 1$^1/_2$ in. (4 cm) Ø	round, tile red	59 (150)	Fox rose. Prone to disease. Strong scent. "Bicolor"—outside yellow, inside red: Capuchin rose.
Rosa hemisphaerica Herrm.	Turkey	sulfur yellow, 2–2$^1/_4$ in. (5–6 cm) Ø	round, dark red	39–78 (100–200)	Double flowers, easily damaged by rain, a rarity.
Rosa hugonis Hemsley	Central China	light yellow, very early, 2 in. (5 cm) Ø	fat, round, very dark red	98 (250)	Golden Rose of China. Rewarding early bloomer.
Rosa longicuspis Bertol.	W. China, Himalaya	cream white clusters, late, $^3/_4$–1 in. (2–3 cm) Ø	oval, orange	195 (500)	Vigorously growing climber, shining green leaves. Somewhat vulnerable to frost.
Rosa oxyodon Boiss.	E. Caucasus	dark pink, 2$^1/_4$ in. (6 cm) Ø	red, bottle-shaped	78–117 (200–300)	Beautiful flowers and fruits.
Rosa primula Bouleng.	Turkestan to China	light yellow, 1 in. (3 cm) Ø, early	round, scarlet	78 (200)	7–13 leaflets, should stand alone, often the earliest rose.
Rosa setigera Michx.	N. America	dark rose 2$^1/_4$ in. (6 cm) Ø, late	round, small, brown green	59–78 (150–200)	"Prairie rose." Beautiful flowers.
Rosa setipoda Hemsl. & Wils.	Central China	rosy purple to rose, 2 in. (5 cm) Ø	bottle-shaped, red	156–195 (400–500)	Large thorns, outstand-ingly thick purply canes.
Rosa stellata var. mirifica Cockerell	New Mexico	dark rose to purple, 2 in. (5 cm) Ø, repeats bloom	round, bristly, dull red	35 (90)	Sacramento rose, also "gooseberry" rose because of similar leaf form.
Rosa virginiana Mill.	Eastern N. America	light pink, late, 1$^1/_2$ in. (4 cm) Ø	flattened round, $^1/_2$ in. (1.5 cm) Ø, red	59–78 (150–200)	Robust wild rose, also embankment rose.
Rosa x kordesii Wulff.	Grower W. Kordes 1942	red to light red, semidouble, 3 in. (8 cm) Ø	oval, late-ripening	98 (250)	Species-hybrid. Beginning species for many climbing and shrub roses.
Rosa x paulii Rehd.	Bred before 1903	white, 2$^1/_4$–2$^3/_4$ in. (6–7 cm) Ø	—	78–156 (200–400)	Hybrid. Ground cover, very vigorous grower, arched creeping (Syn. = *Rosa rugosa* "Repens alba").
Rosa x pteragonis Krause	Bred 1938	light yellow, 2 in. (5 cm) Ø	—	78 (200)	Hybrid. "Red Wing" a very beautiful related Krause variety.
Rosa x richardii Rehd.	Bred Ethiopia 1897	silvery light pink, 2$^1/_4$–2$^3/_4$ in. (6–7 cm) Ø, urn-shaped	—	27 (70)	= *Rosa sancta,* Holy Rose. Hybrid, probably *Rosa gallica x Rosa phoenicea.*
Rosa x waitziana Tratt.	Bred 1874	dark rose 2$^3/_4$ in. (7 cm) Ø	fall, off green	78 (200)	Hybrid. From *Rosa canina x Rosa gallica.* Coarse foliage.
Rosa xanthina Lindl.	N. China, Korea	golden yellow, very early, 2 in. (5 cm) Ø, semidouble	—	59–117 (150–300)	Wild species is *Rosa xanthina f. spontanea.* From it, varieties like "Golden Wings."

CLIMBING ROSES

Climbers are the biggest magicians in the garden. Within a few years the emptiest corner can be transformed into a fairy-tale Sleeping Beauty bower.

We distinguish these varieties

• according to the way the flowers grow. Most climbers flower either in dense clusters or else deck themselves with single large flowers and thus fit into either the cluster-flowering or the large-flowered bedding rose categories.

• according to the frequency of flowering. There are some among them that bloom only once, as well as repeat-flowering varieties.

• according to the manner of growth. The English have long distinguished between "ramblers" and "climbers." The following portrait section is arranged by these classifications.

Ramblers

The rambler classification includes all climbing roses that have thin or soft, creeping or hanging canes. All hybrids go back to the wild roses with rambler characteristics like *Rosa arvensis, Rosa multiflora, Rosa wichuraiana, Rosa moschata.* These wild roses literally entwine their surroundings or creep into fine-branched bushes, eventually covering them completely.

All ramblers—also their varieties—have the following in common (with a few exceptions): They bloom only once, in clusters of small flowers. There are scarcely any yellow shades. Their leaves are small to medium in size. They are quite healthy. They need a support to climb very high.

Climbers

These roses have stout, vigorous canes, often branching, spreading climbers that grow upright and hook in with thorns in order to gain height. They can reach from 6–13 ft (2–4 m) even without support.

Handling Climbers

• Plant climbers with the bud union 2–3 in. (5–8 cm) under the soil surface.

• Protect them in winter (see page 39).

• See page 43 for how to prune climbers properly.

If in spite of these precautions a climbing rose sustains serious frost damage, it will come back again after three years at the latest.

Two ramblers in comparison. "The Garland" (right) blooms semidouble and fragrant in long, densely filled, well-arranged garlands. Behind it "Bobbie James" (left) climbs into a locust over 23 ft (7 m) high and hangs way down low.

CLIMBING ROSES

Sympathie
Kordes 1964, ADR Rose 1966.
Buds large, roundish oval. Flowers velvety dark red; large-flowered; 4 in. (11 cm) Ø very double; hybrid-tea-like, alone or in cluster; good fragrance. Very heavy bloomer, good repeat-flowering until fall. Durable and rainfast. Almost round, red orange hips, $^3/_4$ in. (2 cm) Ø, of moderate decorative value. Growth very vigorous, over 195 in. (500 cm) tall, with sturdy, stiff canes, outspreading. Foliage medium-sized, lush green, shining. Use for pergolas, summerhouses, walls, high gables and balconies, rose arbors.

My tip: Spot anthracnose common in late summer. The baring of the lower sections can be counter-acted by staged pruning of the weakest one-year-old bottom canes—to 23, 35, and 51 in. (60, 90, and 130 cm) in height. Alternative: Plant less vigorously growing blue clematis, perennials, or grasses in front of it. Not suitable for a cascade rose. Heavy feeder.

Direktor Benschop
(= "City of York")
Tantau 1945.
Buds classic; medium size, greenish-white. Flowers creamy white; medium size at $2^3/_4$ in. (7 cm) Ø, semidouble, 15 petals, with yellow stamens; with 3–10 in clusters, good scent. Blooms very heavily but only once. Lasting. Sometimes numerous hips, $^1/_2$ in. (1.5 cm) Ø, round, yellow orange, moderate decorative value. Growth vigorous, 156 to 234 in. (400–600 cm) tall. Foliage dark green, shining, leathery, medium-sized. Use for trellises, walls, arbors, pergolas, pillars, and other structures for climbing.

Sympathie

My tip: Canes somewhat vulnerable to frost; winter protection. They are easy to direct by tying.

Compassion
Harkness 1971, ADR Rose 1976.
Buds large, pointed round, yellow red. Flowers salmon orange and copper gold to silvery pink; resemble hybrid tea and are large-flowered, 4 to almost 5 in. (10–12 cm) Ø, fully but loosely doubled, with 25 petals; with outstanding intense

Direktor Benschop

Compassion

Flammentanz

Goldener Olymp

New Dawn

fragrance. Repeats bloom—with pauses—very well. <u>Growth</u> as climbing rose only vigorous enough on good soil, 117 in. (300 cm) high. Broadly bushy. Canes stiff, but hardly any loss of foliage at bottom. <u>Foliage</u> large, coarse, very thick, dark green, glossy. The leaves go very well with the interesting color play of the flowers. <u>Use</u> for trellises, pillars, hedges. Also can be used as a large solitary shrub rose, but then space more than 98 in. (250 cm) apart.

My tip: Healthy, but often freezes back.

Flammentanz
Kordes 1955, ADR Rose 1952.
<u>Buds</u> fat, round, very dark red. <u>Flowers</u> dark red to bloodred; medium-sized, $3^1/_2$ in. (9 cm) Ø. They are loosely double, with 25 petals, and occur in clusters. Little scent. Blooms only once—however, very lushly. The flowers hold for a very long time and turn blue just at the end. It is quite rainfast

and self-cleaning. Hips are oval to round, over $^3/_4$ in. (2 cm) Ø, of great decorative value. <u>Growth</u> very stiff, 156–195 in. (400–500 cm) high—nevertheless, also very green at the bottom. <u>Foliage</u> large, leathery, matte green. <u>Use</u> for pergolas, trellises, walls, and arbors.

My tip: Probably by a wide margin the frost-hardiest climbing rose of this type; also for tough locations.

Goldener Olymp
Kordes 1984.
Buds pointed-cone-shaped, large, yellow orange. Flowers golden yellow; large, $3^1/_2$ in. (9 cm) Ø, very double, with 30 petals. Flowers occur several together; fragrant. Flowers frequently until frost. <u>Growth</u> vigorous, branching and bushy, upright, stiff, 98 in. (250 cm) tall. <u>Foliage</u> medium-sized, lush, shining, deep-green. <u>Use</u> for arbors, pergolas, small walls, pillars. <u>Also recommended:</u> "<u>Goldstern</u>" by Tantau 1966, a now time-tested variety, which grows even more vigorously. Height 117 in. (300 cm). "<u>Golden Showers</u>" by Lammerts 1958 has mostly single, hybrid-tea-type flowers on long stems and furthermore is quite healthy.

My tip: Suitable as a shrub rose.

New Dawn
Somerset Nursery 1930.
<u>Buds</u> pointed oval, pale pink. <u>Flowers</u> pale pink; 3 in. (8 cm) Ø; loosely double with 20 petals. Hybrid-tea-like, medium-sized flowers, usually in clusters, with fine scent. Reblooms well in late summer in clusters at the ends of long canes. Quite rainfast, self-cleaning. <u>Growth</u> vigorous, 156 in. (400 cm) high, arching and spreading wide. Canes medium-sturdy, elegant, stiff at the bottom at first. <u>Foliage</u> small with roundish leaves, light green at first, then deep green, shining. <u>Use</u> as winter-hardy rose for pergolas, trellises, arbors, and also for hanging over walls.

My tip: Occasionally mildew in the fall, nevertheless one of our best climbing roses. Just after the first flowering, cut off the faded clusters. Good as a high cascade rose. World-renowned.

CLIMBING ROSES

Veilchenblau
J. C. Schmidt 1909.
Buds small and round, deep crimson. Flowers crimson violet with whitish eye, later blue violet; small-flowered, 1 in. (3 cm) Ø; single or semidouble, flowering very heavily in large clusters, often very fragrant. Blooms once, quite early. Growth very vigorous, with many light green, almost thornless canes, up-right rambler-type, 195 in. (500 cm) high. Foliage light green, elongated, very healthy. Use for gazebos, pergolas, arbors, walls, pillars, trees. Also recommended: Almost identical is "Donau," Prascac 1913. Flowers a bit larger, good scent. A little bit more intense in color, crimson violet, but very double—like a pompom—is "Améthyste" by Nonin 1911; otherwise similar but somewhat less vigorous in growth.

My tip: "Veilchenblau" is quite frost-hardy. Plant together with "Madeleine Seltzer," which comes into bloom only slightly earlier.

Kiftsgate
E. Murrel 1954.
Selection or sport of *Rosa filipes*.
Buds small, roundish. Flowers cream white; small, less than 1 in. (3 cm) Ø, growing in large panicles; good fragrance. Flowers late and particularly heavily, regrettably only once. With marvelous bunches of long-lasting, small, oval-round, deep orange-red hips in fall. Growth extremely vigorous, canes up to 234 in. (600 cm) in one year. Foliage medium-sized, light green, very shiny until late fall. Use to twine over large old trees (pines), walls, pergolas, gazebos. Also recommended: *Rosa multiflora* "Carnea," "Paul's Himalayan Musk Rambler," "Lykkefund," "The Garland" (with hips).

Veilchenblau

Kiftsgate

American Pillar

Madeleine Seltzer

My tip: Considered vulnerable to frost; therefore better in mild regions.

American Pillar
Van Fleet 1902.
Buds roundish, usually in large clusters. Flowers crimson pink with white eye; medium-sized, 2 in. (6 cm) Ø; single, open saucer flower with yellow stamens, in bunches on sturdy stems; no scent. Very heavy bloomer but only once, in June/July. Growth very strong, but weak canes, rambler-type, 117–195 in. (300–500 cm) high, arching and overhanging. Foliage dark green, glossy. Use in cooler, airy locations, only freestanding on pillars, arbors, and pergolas.

My tip: Rather susceptible to mildew. Don't use on a house wall.

98

Rambling Rector

Maria Lisa

Rambling Rector
England before 1910.
<u>Buds</u> small, roundish. <u>Flowers</u> creamy white; small, 1 in. (3 cm) Ø, semidouble, stamens golden yellow; many single flowers occur in clusters; intense fragrance. Once-blooming. <u>Growth</u> densely branching, 156 in. (400 cm) high. <u>Foliage</u> medium green, medium-sized, elegant. <u>Use</u> for arbors, trellises, and pergolas; also suitable to entwine with bushes and trees.

Maria Lisa
Brümmer 1925/Liebau 1936.
<u>Buds</u> small, round. <u>Flowers</u> bright red, white inside; small, $^1/_2$ to 1 in. (1.5–2.5 cm) Ø, but very numerous in panicles; single, once-blooming, therefore very heavy, with an effect like a bright red *Rosa multiflora;* no scent. Flowers keep a long time. Small hips, less than $^1/_2$ in. (1 cm) Ø, red, fat, pear-shaped. <u>Growth</u> rambler type, overhanging, vigorous, 117 in. (300 cm) high, thornless. <u>Foliage</u> small, medium green. <u>Use</u> as pillar, for walls, pergolas, arbors, also on trees.
   My tip: Very suitable for cascade roses, but grows rather wide. Somewhat vulnerable to frost, not recommended for harsh locations.

Madeleine Seltzer
Walter 1926.
<u>Buds</u> roundish, medium-sized. <u>Flowers</u> lemon yellow to white; medium-sized, 3 in. (8 cm) Ø, double with 25 petals, in dense clusters; attractive, highly visible golden yellow stamens; fragrant. Blooms once and early. <u>Growth</u> medium strong, upright rambler-type, over 117 in. (300 cm) high; red canes, almost thornless. <u>Foliage</u> bronze green, medium-sized. <u>Use</u> for walls, pergolas, pillars, arbors, summerhouses.
   My tip: Very frost-hardy. Very beautiful used together with "Veilchenblau."

CLIMBING ROSES

Super Excelsa

Hetzel 1986, ADR Rose 1991.
Buds small, oval, red. Flowers crimson pink with white center stripe, bluish with purple shades as they fade; 1 in. (3 cm) Ø, densely double, pompom-like, 25 petals that become smaller and smaller toward the center. Quite dense, many-flowered, round-clustered inflorescences; no scent. Reblooms well after an initial pause; rainfast to some extent. Growth only moderately strong; thin, soft, rambler canes, recumbent, when tied up, 59–98 in. (150–250 cm) high. Foliage seven leaflets, small, light green at first, then medium green, glossy. Use only for small pillars and small walls, since the numerous flowers hinder longer annual cane growth, very good as a cascade rose and as a ground cover. Also recommended: "Super Dorothy," pink, and "Hermann Schmidt," lavender-crimson. Neither much troubled by mildew.

Gruss an Zabern

Lambert 1904.
Buds round, medium-sized, cream-colored. Flowers pure white with a little cream tone; medium-sized, 2 in. (6 cm) Ø, doubled rosettes with 30 petals, in dense clusters; fragrant. Flowers only once, therefore super-abundantly and very early. Growth good medium vigor, over 117 in. (300 cm) high; rambler type with dense branching. Foliage small, longish-oval leaflets, dark green. Use for gazebos, pillars, fences, pergolas, small walls, and as a cascade rose.
   My tip: Quite frost-hardy. Utilize its early flowering for your needs. Really healthy, elegant growth habit.

Super Excelsa

Albéric Barbier

Barbier 1900.
Buds medium-sized, slender, classic, yellow. Flowers yellowish at first, then almost white with cream-colored centers; loosely double, 3 in. (8 cm) Ø, star-shaped, classic; situated singly, rarely in groups of several, good fragrance. Once-blooming. Growth very vigorous, spreads to over 195 in. (500 cm); descended from *Rosa luciae,* rambler type with relatively soft canes that are red when young. Foliage dark green, outstandingly glossy, very decorative, almost evergreen. Use for pillars, pergolas, gazebos, arbors, and cascade roses on standards over 59 in. (150 cm) high. Because of the weak canes, it might also be tried as an embankment planting or as ground cover, spaced 55 in. (140 cm) apart.
   My tip: To avoid mildew, don't plant on hot walls. Admirers treasure the singly growing flowers against the dark leaves and the vigorous growth habit.

Gruss an Zabern

Albéric Barbier

Albertine

Venusta Pendula

Bobbie James

Venusta Pendula
Rosa arvensis hybrid of unknown origin.
Reintroduced by W. Kordes 1928.
<u>Buds</u> small, spherical, with many in one cluster. <u>Flowers</u> pale pink, later almost white; at 1$\frac{1}{2}$ in. (4 cm) Ø, small-flowered, loosely semidouble, 12 petals; without scent; blooms very heavily but only once. Single globular hips. <u>Growth</u> very strong, up to 234 in. (600 cm) high; weak, thin, overhanging or pendant canes, do not lose leaves. <u>Foliage</u> medium-sized, reddish green, dull; some fall coloring to yellow. <u>Use</u> for gazebos and pergolas.
   My tip: The lush flowers and the elegant growth habit make this rose versatile for many purposes, even in semishade.

Bobbie James
Sunningdale Nurseries 1961.
<u>Buds</u> creamy white, small, round in large clusters. <u>Flowers</u> creamy white to white; small, 1 in. (3 cm) Ø, with 5–8 petals, just barely doubled, shallowly saucer-shaped; delicate fragrance. Blooms very lushly in large clusters; once-flowering. Oval, dark red hips, up to 20 in loose bunches. <u>Growth</u> extremely vigorous, over 273 in. (700 cm) high; a few sharp, hook-shaped thorns; upright rambler. <u>Foliage</u> light to medium green, somewhat glossy. <u>Use</u> for trees, gazebos, pergolas, walls.
   My tip: Despite its vigor and luxuriant growth, this rose is still not suitable for harsh conditions. However, it will bloom in part shade.
<u>Note:</u> For more good climbing roses, see pages 150–153.

Albertine
Wichuraiana hybrid. Barbier 1921.
<u>Buds</u> salmon-colored, pointed oval. <u>Flowers</u> pastel apricot pink; medium-sized, 3 in. (8 cm) Ø, loosely doubled with 20 petals; growing alone or in bunches of several; strongly scented. Blooms only once, but generally very lushly. <u>Growth</u> very sturdy, up to 156 in. (400 cm) high, branching shrublike. <u>Foliage</u> dark green, matte. <u>Use</u> for freestanding trellises, pillars, arbors, pergolas.
   My tip: To prevent spot anthracnose, fertilize in May with horn meal, so that new canes will come up healthy. A nostalgic variety, not for harsh conditions. Beautiful for cut flowers.

CLIMBING ROSES

Variety	Grower/Year	Flower	Height in in. (cm)	Comments
Climbers—Varieties with Strong Canes				
Alexandre Girault	Barbier 1909	crimson rose red, 2^1/$_4$ in. (6 cm) Ø, double, blooms once	156 (400)	Quite robust, some mildew, strong growth.
Clair Matin	Meilland 1960	pale pink, 3 in. (8 cm) Ø, semidouble, repeat-blooming	to 117 (300)	Fragrant, very luxuriant, some mildew. Stiff canes.
Dortmund	Kordes 1955	bloodred, white eye, 4 in. (10 cm) Ø, single, repeat-blooming, in clusters	137 (350)	ADR Rose 1954, prevent setting of hips. Some fragrance.
Ilse Krohn Superior	Kordes 1957	white, 4 in. (10 cm) Ø, double, repeat-blooming	117 (300)	Repeats well.
Long John Silver	Horvarth 1934	white, 4 in. (10 cm) Ø, blooms once	156 (400)	Fragrant. Saucer-shaped flowers in large clusters.
Mme Grégoire Staechelin	Dot 1927	bright red to pink, 4^1/$_4$ in. (11 cm) Ø, double, blooms once	117–156 (300–400)	Very large, pear-shaped orange hips with great decorative value.
Mme Sancy de Parabère	Bonnet 1874	rose pink, 4^3/$_4$ in. (12 cm) Ø, double, blooms once	to 156 (400)	Thornless canes, very early. Some fragrance.
Morletti	Morlet 1883	magenta pink, 3 in. (8 cm) Ø, loosely double, blooms once	117 (300)	Thornless, hardly any scent, frost-hardy, abundant bloom, fall coloration.
Parade	Boerner/Jackson & Perkins 1953	deep pink, 3½ in. (9 cm) Ø, semidouble, repeat-blooming	117–156 (300–400)	Fragrant. Form and color go well with old roses.
Paul's Scarlet Climber	Paul 1915	red, 3 in. (8 cm) Ø, semidouble, blooms once	117–195 (300–500)	Also good as a shrub rose.
Rosenresli	Kordes 1982	dark pink, 3½ in. (9 cm) Ø, double, repeat-blooming	78 (200)	ADR Rose 1984, strong scent, also as shrub.
Salita	Kordes 1987	orange, 4 in. (10 cm) Ø, double repeat-blooming	78 (200)	Luxuriant bloomer; also as shrub rose.
Schneewalzer	Tantau 1987	white, 4^1/$_4$ in. (11 cm) Ø, double repeat-blooming	98 (250)	Slow-growing.
Schwarzer Samt	v. Teschendorf AG 1969	very dark red, 4 in. (10 cm) Ø, loosely double, repeat-blooming	98 (250)	Also good as shrub.
Till Uhlenspiegel	Kordes 1950	red with white center, 3 in. (8 cm) Ø, single, blooms once	to 117 (300)	Overhanging branches.
White Cockade	Cocker 1969	white, outsides slightly reddish, 3½ in. (9 cm) Ø, double, repeat blooming	78 (200)	Abundant flowers in clusters.
Zéphirine Drouhin	Bizot 1868	pink with white center, 4 in. (10 cm) Ø, semidouble, repeat-blooming	to 117 (300)	Bourbon rose, fragrant, thornless, some mildew.

Variety	Grower/Year	Flower	Height in in. (cm)	Comments

Ramblers—Varieties with Weak Canes

Variety	Grower/Year	Flower	Height in in. (cm)	Comments
Apple Blossom	Burbank 1932	pale pink, 1½ in. (4 cm) Ø, single, blooms once	195 (500)	Quite robust, very beautiful, luxuriant flowers in large clusters.
Blush Rambler	B. R. Cant 1903	light pink, 1 in. (3 cm) Ø, semidouble, blooms once	117–156 (300–400)	Fragrant, flowers luxuriantly in large clusters.
Bonfire	Turbat 1928	red, 1½ in. (4 cm) Ø, double, blooms once	to 195 (500)	Not to be confused with the floribunda rose of the same name.
Crimson Rambler	Turner 1893	bright red, 1 in. (3 cm) Ø, very double, blooms once	195–234 (500–600)	Luxuriant bloom, mildew in late summer.
Easlea's Golden Rambler	Easlea 1932	lemon yellow, 4 in. (10 cm) Ø, double, blooms once	156 (400)	Relatively stiff growth, some spot anthracnose.
François Juranville	Barbier 1906	salmon pink, 4 in. (10 cm) Ø, loosely doubled, blooms once	195–234 (500–600)	Sweet scent. Little mildew.
Frl. Octavia Hesse	Hesse 1909	yellowish white, 2¼ in. (6 cm) Ø, double, blooms once	234 (600)	Fragrant, foliage glossy, disposed to mildew, spot anthracnose.
Ghislaine de Féligonde	Turbat 1916	pink to ivory, 3 in. (8 cm) Ø, loosely doubled, blooms once	78–117 (200–300)	Somewhat sensitive.
Hermann Schmidt	Hetzel 1986	purple crimson, 1 in. (3 cm) Ø, very double, repeat-blooming	117 (300)	Pompom-like flowers, second flowering quite good.
Hiawatha	Walsh 1904	crimson with white center, 2 in. (5 cm) Ø, semi-double, blooms once	156 (400)	Late-blooming, somewhat delicate.
Kew Rambler	Kew 1912	salmon pink, center lighter, 1 in. (2.5 cm) Ø, single, blooms once	234 (600)	Vigorous grower, climbs well in trees, large flower clusters.
Lykkefund	Olsen 1930	cream white, 1½ in. (4 cm) Ø, almost single, blooms once	156–234 (400–600)	Climbs well in trees, healthy, frost-hardy, large, fragrant panicles.
Paul Noël	Tanne 1913	apricot pink, 2¾ in. (7 cm) Ø, double, repeat blooming	117 (300)	Some scent, luxuriant flowers, bushy growth, healthy.
Paul's Himalayan Musk	Paul c. 1890	lavender pink and white, 1–1½ in. (3–4 cm) Ø, repeat-blooming	234 (600)	Romantic, cluster-flowered rambler of particular delicacy.
Polstjärnan	Wasastjärna 1937	white, 2¼ in. (6 cm) Ø, almost single, blooms once	over 195 (500)	Some repeat-blooming in late summer, very winter-hardy.
Russeliana	c. 1840	purplish red, 1½ in. (4 cm) Ø, double, blooms once	to 234 (600)	Heavy flowering.
Super Dorothy	Hetzel 1986	pink, 1 in. (3 cm) double, repeat-blooming	117 (300)	Pompom-like flowers, little tendency to mildew.
Tausendschön	Kiese/J. C. Schmidt 1906	pink, white center, 1½ in. (4 cm) Ø, very double, blooms once	117 (300)	Heavy flowering, thornless.

Portraits
SHRUB ROSES

Among the shrub roses there are single- and double-flowered varieties of all sizes and colors. The most important subdivision is between roses that flower once and those that repeat, and pruning differs accordingly (see KNOW-HOW: Pruning, pages 42–43).

Once-flowering shrub roses are still occasionally called park roses, although they are also appropriate for gardens.

Modern Shrub Roses
These have been called modern shrub roses, since hybrid teas were crossed with the already recognized shrub roses about 100 years ago. Their most beautiful representatives can be seen on pages 106 to 109.

Old Roses
Damask and Gallica roses, see pages 110–111. These are almost all once-flowering and are considered the oldest roses.

Portland and Bourbon roses often bloom again slightly in late summer, see pages 112–113.

Centifolia roses with the subgroup Moss Roses, see pages 114–115. They probably appeared around 1600 in the low countries.

China and Noisette roses, see pages 116–117, have the genes of the China roses and thus are repeat-blooming.

Hybrid Perpetual roses, Lambertiana roses, and Musk hybrids, see pages 118–119. These all bloom more than once.

The hybrid perpetuals developed with the participation of many rose groups: Portland and Bourbon roses, Noisette and tea roses, thus the repeat-blooming China roses. They are recognized by their robust growth and their strong colors. What from today's point of view is only moderate repeat-flowering in late summer (and after a long hiatus) appeared at the time of their breeding to be a tremendous step forward. The name "hybrid perpetual" reflects that. They are also sometimes called "remontant" roses, which means "blooming more often." However, this name wasn't precisely accurate until the creation of the hybrid tea, polyantha, and floribunda roses. The transition from the hybrid perpetuals to the modern hybrid teas and shrub roses was swift.

English Roses
See pages 120–121. These modern developments by the English grower David Austin seek to join the charms of the old roses with the virtues of modern varieties. They are mostly in gentle pastel colors, possess very double flowers, often with an entrancing fragrance. Nevertheless many of them bloom repeatedly and are of good hardiness.

The English shrub rose "Graham Thomas" from grower David Austin here has a carpet of catnip, *Nepeta x fassenii*, at its base.

SHRUB ROSES

Dirigent
Tantau 1956, ADR-Rose 1958.
<u>Buds</u> round-oval, medium-sized, dark red. <u>Flowers</u> brilliant bloodred; medium-sized, $2^3/_4$ in. (7 cm) Ø; semidouble with about 15 to 25 petals, growing in large clusters; blooms until late fall; self-cleaning. <u>Growth</u> broad, bushy, upright, about 59–78 in. (150–200 cm) high and 39–47 in. (100–120 cm) wide. <u>Foliage</u> large, medium green, slightly glossy. <u>Use</u> singly or in groups, free standing or in shrub plantings, or as an everblooming hedge.

My tip: Somewhat susceptible to spot anthracnose.

Freisinger Morgenröte
Kordes 1988.
<u>Buds</u> oval to cone-shaped, coppery yellow red. <u>Flowers</u> orange on yellow background; medium-sized, 3 in. (8 cm) Ø, with yellow petals, several in a cluster, fragrant; very luxuriant bloomer until frost. <u>Growth</u> upright, broad, bushy, stiff, well-branched, 59 in. (150 cm) high. <u>Foliage</u> medium to dark green, leathery, robust. <u>Use</u> alone or in small groups, also good as hedge.

My tip: In some years, spot anthracnose appears. The amber-colored "Westfalenpark" combines with other flowers more easily than "Freisinger Morgenröte" because of its more restrained coloring.

Westerland
Kordes 1969, ADR Rose 1974.
<u>Buds</u> pointed oval, copper red with yellow, up to 10 in a loose bunch. <u>Flowers</u> amber yellow with fiery orange red, bordered with orange to apricot; large-flowered, 4–5 in. (10–12 cm) Ø, loosely double with 20–25 somewhat wavy petals. Pleasing scent. Early and lushly

Dirigent

blooming until frost. Orange hips with decorative value, flattish round, $^1/_2$ in. (1.5 cm) Ø. <u>Growth</u> strong, almost broader than high, 78 in. (200 cm). Well-branched, at first upright, soon broadly spreading shrub, which appears compact with its closely growing, large leaves. <u>Foliage</u> reddish when new, then deep green, glossy, leathery. <u>Use</u> in single settings or as a lone group is very impressive. The beautiful amber orange color play is hard to coordinate with plants of other colors. Plant 78 in. (200 cm) apart.

My tip: Healthy, but occasionally spot anthracnose appears. Summer pruning more advisable than display of hips.

Freisinger Morgenröte

Westerland

Grandhotel

Lichtkönigin Lucia

Fontaine

Grandhotel
MacGredy 1972, ADR Rose 1977.
Buds thick, pointed oval, red, often in clusters. Flowers velvety scarlet, later bloodred; hybrid-tea shape, large, 4 in. (10 cm) Ø, double, 25 petals, no scent. Repeat-flowering until October, weatherfast. Growth strong, over 78 in. (200 cm), puts out new growth until fall, thus bushy, 59 in. (150 cm) wide. Foliage large, thick; reddish at first, then dark green, very glossy. Use in our climate as a vigorous shrub rose, even a climber; alone and in groups; 78 in. (200 cm) apart.
   My tip: Cut off fading flowers to promote more flowers rather than hips.

Lichtkönigin Lucia
Kordes 1966, ADR Rose 1968.
Buds large, oval, hybrid-tea shape, several together, intense yellow. Flowers blazing bright yellow to lemon yellow; large 3–4 in. (8–10 cm) Ø, quite double, 20–25 petals, short-stemmed. Red stamens create a golden yellow shimmer in the center. Some fragrance. A wealth of flowers, beginning early and blooming steadily well up until fall. Flowers keep a long time, at the end somewhat lighter in the sun. Growth strong, very stiffly upright, almost compact; narrow interval between leaves, 59 in. (150 cm) high. Foliage large, at first light green, then deep green, leathery, ridged, glossy. Use as very good solitary or group rose, also suitable for small gardens. Good in front of dark green hedges and with shrubs. Distance 47 in. (120 cm) apart.

Fontaine
(= "Fountain")
Tantau 1970, ADR Rose 1971.
Buds pointed-oval, slender, hybrid-tea shape, dark red, growing alone or a few together. Flowers brilliant velvety bloodred, good color consistency. It can burn in hot sun; large-flowered, but loosely double, 4–5 in. (10–12 cm) Ø, 20 petals. Free-flowering, long-lasting, and good repeat-blooming right up until frost; rainfast. Growth vigorous, upright, 59 in. (150 cm) high; adequate branching, bushy. Foliage large, reddish at first, then dark-green, dull, dense. Use alone or as a group rose. Space 47 in. (120 cm) apart.
   My tip: Susceptible to spot anthracnose from August on. Also useful as a cut rose.

SHRUB ROSES

Schneewittchen
(= "Iceberg," "Fee des Neiges")
Kordes 1958, ADR Rose 1960,
World Rose 1983.
<u>Buds</u> long and pointed, greenish white to rosy white; 3–7 occur together in loose clusters. <u>Flowers</u> pure white, rosy in cold; medium-sized, $2^3/_4$–3 in. (7–8 cm) Ø, loosely double, 25 petals, saucer-shaped with open center, yellow stamens very visible. Good fragrance. Copiously and constantly flowering, with vigorous late fall bloom; rainfast, self-cleaning. <u>Growth</u> moderate, upright, 47 in. (120 cm) high, often archingly overhanging. Light green canes with few thorns. <u>Foliage</u> medium-sized, leaflets slender with clearly extended tips, light green to medium green, somewhat glossy. <u>Use</u> in groups but also as hedge, alone, even as a higher-growing bedding rose with hard annual pruning. Space 35 in. (90 cm) apart.
My tip: Not very frost-hardy. Spot anthracnose possible after August.

Centenaire de Lourdes
Delbard-Chabert 1958.
<u>Buds</u> cone-shaped, bright red, in loose clusters of 5–10. <u>Flowers</u> intense pink, almost luminous bright red in center; medium-sized, 3–$3^1/_2$ in. (8–9 cm) Ø, loosely double, the center closed into a longish ball shape, 15–20 slightly wavy petals; lightly scented. Freely flowering, beginning moderately late, continuous flowering until late August. Hips orange, $^3/_4$ in. (2 cm) Ø, oval. <u>Growth</u> loose and well-branched, moderately overhanging; wider than high; medium strong, 39–59 in. (100–150 cm) high. <u>Foliage</u> very healthy until fall, glossy, medium green. <u>Use</u> as single planting; goes well with shrubs and bushes. Space 51 in. (130 cm) apart.

Schneewittchen

Centenaire de Lourdes

Edenrose '85

Angela

My tip: Ideal combined with "Schneewittchen," delphinium, madonna lilies. Remains healthy during dry spells. Don't encourage formation of hips at the expense of better repeat-flowering; always cut off spent flower clusters. A topnotch variety.

Edenrose '85
Meilland/Strobel 1986.
<u>Buds</u> globular, large. <u>Flowers</u> pale pink, paling faintly toward the edges like silk, become an intense rose toward the center; large-flowered, $^3/_4$ in. (12 cm) Ø, very double; the more than 60 petals are rainfast. The heavy flowers often nod. The almost ball-shaped flower center unfolds luxuriously in the style of the centifolia flower; hardly any scent. Reblooms very well. <u>Growth</u> sturdy, overhanging with heavy burden of flowers and fully bushy, well-branched, and continuous new growth. <u>Foliage</u> large, dense, sturdy, leathery, dark-green, with some gloss. <u>Use</u> as single planting or in groups, also as shrub or

Modern Varieties

Erfurt

Nevada

Erfurt
Kordes 1939.

<u>Buds</u> oval, pointed, bright red. <u>Flowers</u> yellowish white in center, gradually becoming crimson toward the edges, intense in cool weather and semishade, somewhat lighter in the sun. Stamens yellow. Large-flowered, 4–4³/₄ in. (10–12 cm) Ø, semidouble to single, saucer-shaped. Freely flowering, very good continued flowering right up until fall if beginnings of hips are removed before they develop. Hips are without decorative value, orange red, 1 in. (2.5 cm) Ø, round. <u>Growth</u> vigorous, spreading and overhanging, 39–59 in. (100–150 cm) high. <u>Foliage</u> darkgreen, new growth dark red. Healthy foliage. <u>Use</u> as single planting in front of shrubs, good with perennials. Plant 39 in. (100 cm) apart.

Nevada
P. Dot 1927.

Rosa moyesii hybrid.

<u>Buds</u> oval, pointed; pink or apricot. <u>Flowers</u> creamy white; very large, 4³/₄ in. (12 cm), shallow, single to semidouble with 5–10 slightly wavy petals; beautiful yellow stamens; little scent. Blooms twice, the first flowering very early and heavy, the second in August noticeably weaker. Self-cleaning, no fruits. <u>Growth</u> in stories, very outspread, reaches a good 78 in. (200 cm) in height. <u>Foliage</u> light green, dull, faintly graytoned. <u>Use</u> as early-blooming single planting, distance 98 in. (250 cm). <u>Also recommended:</u> "<u>Marguerite Hilling</u>," Hilling 1959. (= "Pink Nevada"), sport of "Nevada." Pure pink flowers.

My tip: Plant both varieties together. That way the flow of flowers never stops; prune back radically every 6–8 years to 4 in. (10 cm) above the ground.

Angela
Kordes 1984, ADR Rose 1982.

<u>Buds</u> numerous, cone-shaped, small. <u>Flowers</u> intense rose; medium-sized, 2 in. (6 cm) Ø, semidouble, 15 petals, arranged in clusters, freely flowering until fall, rainfast. <u>Growth</u> sturdy, upright, well-branched, somewhat overhanging. Forms large, round, self-contained bushes of 62 in. (160 cm) in height and 59 in. (150 cm) in breadth. <u>Foliage</u> medium-sized, glossy green. <u>Use</u> as single planting, also as space-filler or hedges, at intervals of 39 in. (100 cm). <u>Also recommended:</u> "<u>Carola</u>," Noack 1988.

My tip: Some spot anthracnose, only in fall. Winter-hardy.

along fence. Space 98 in. (250 cm) apart.

My tip: Remove shriveled buds after rain. A rose with an antique effect but full of vigor.

SHRUB ROSES

Madame Zoetmans
Damask rose. Marest 1830.
Flowers pale pink, finally almost white with a beautiful green eye; large, 4 in. (10 cm) Ø; 30 petals, saucer-shaped, occasionally quartered like the centifolias, usually in clusters of several, well distributed; very pleasing fragrance. Growth upright, good, shrubby branching, agreeable form, 47 in. (120 cm) high. Foliage medium to dark green, lush. Use as a small shrub by itself or in groups, too low for hedges. Space 51 in. (130 cm) apart. Also recommended: The few Damask garden varieties are more attractive than the one used for rose-oil production, *Rosa x damascena* "Trigintipetala" or "Kasanlik" (synonym), which has a sprawling growth habit. An interesting one is *Rosa x damascena* "Versicolor," also known as the "York and Lancaster" rose; irregular pale pink and white, sometimes flecked, semidouble; good scent.

Charles de Mills
Gallica shrub rose.
Unknown origin.
Flowers dark purplish red to violet red, occasionally with delicate, whitish, arched, fringed petal edges; shallow, fully double with over 40 petals, quartered flowers, 3¹/₂ in. (9 cm) Ø; the outer petals arranged in the form of a circle; a green eye is sometimes visible in the center; marvelous fragrance, once-blooming. Growth markedly roundly bushy, moderately vigorous, 51 in. (130 cm) high, compact. Foliage robust, dark green. Use as medium-sized shrub rose for good soil, tolerates some semishade. Distance 62 in. (160 cm) apart, closer in hedges.

Madame Zoetmans

My tip: One of the best Gallica roses. Since most old roses are white and pink, the darker color tones of the many Gallica roses enjoy special attention.

Rosa gallica "Officinalis"
Red Rose of Lancaster, Apothecary rose, Provence rose. Existence in France in 1310 documented.
Flowers light crimson; medium-sized, 2³/₄ in. (7 cm) Ø, semidouble, 13 petals, beautiful yellow stamens in a little "crown"; flowers occur alone or a few together; very good scent, blooms heavily but only once. Spherical red hips, less than ¹/₂ in. (1 cm) Ø. Growth low, 27 in.

Rosa gallica "Versicolor"

(70 cm) high; dense, round, overhanging bushes. Foliage coarse, medium to dark green, robust. Use as single or group planting, even for low hedges. Good together with perennials. Plant 55 in. (140 cm) apart. Also recommended: *Rosa*

110

Charles de Mills

Rosa gallica "Officinalis"

Celsiana

Rose de Rescht

gallica **"Versicolor,"** also called "Rosa Mundi," with light-pink-and-red-striped flowers.

My tip: Easy-care small shrub rose. Some mildew after flowering. One of the surest old roses, also for smaller gardens. Very good with its sport "Versicolor."

Celsiana
Damask rose. Before 1750.
Flowers lustrous pale pink, fading in full sun; large, 3$^1/_2$ in. (9 cm) Ø, very loosely double, 20 petals, yellow stamens; usually several in gracefully hanging clusters; good scent. Growth roundly shrubby to upright, loosely overhanging, 51 in. (130 cm) high, well-branched, beautiful form. Foliage light green

with gray, soft. Use as single or group planting, in hedge or along fence. Distance 59 in. (150 cm) apart. Also recommended: "Madame Hardy," white, densely double flowers.

My tip: Loose flower forms provide variety in the old roses. Problem-free, beautiful, healthy variety from this attractive scented rose group.

Rose de Rescht
Damask or Portland rose with great similarity to *Rosa gallica.* Cultivated before 1880 in Persia. The uncertainty of its origin, attribution, and introduction to Europe gives this rose a mysterious charm.
Flowers bright crimson, fading to lavender, with shading; small, 2 in. (5 cm) Ø, with over 30 petals, very double, rosette form; flowers well distributed, with several on short stems, close to the dense foliage, blooming one after the other; strong fragrance. Repeat blooming until fall, only brief pause in flowering. Growth uprightly branching, compact, 35 in. (90 cm) high. Foliage large; coarse-plump *Rosa gallica* leaves. Use as small shrub rose alone or in groups, also for low, hedgelike enclosures, with perennials. Distance 39 in. (100 cm) apart.

My tip: Winter-hardy rose. Spot anthracnose, mostly on over-aged branches. One of the best beginner roses. Young, vigorous plants rebloom better, so after 5–6 years do a rejuvenation pruning of old wood. Give it good soil. Abundant fall bloomer. Repeat-flowering is rare in old roses, but very welcome. Grows well on its own roots.

SHRUB ROSES

Madame Boll
Portland rose. Boll/Boyan 1859/60.
Usually mistakenly listed as "Comte de Chambord" commercially. However, this was another, probably quite similar variety.
Flowers rose-colored, overcast with lavender; large, 3 in. (8 cm) Ø, shallow, very double with over 40 petals, quartered in the middle; usually several flowers together on upright stems. Sweet fragrance. Good repeat bloomer. Growth upright, bushy, 39 in. (100 cm) high. Foliage light-green, large, covering well. Use alone or in groups of three, also as accompaniment to perennials.
My tip: One of the best repeat-flowering Portland roses, forms low, round bushes.

Madame Isaac Pereire
Bourbon rose. Garçon 1881.
Flowers crimson rose red with purple; very large, $4^3/_4$ in. (12 cm) Ø, very double with over 40 petals, in lush, closely situated, short-stemmed clusters. The petals roll somewhat stiffly back toward the outside and expose a well-developed flower whorl. Intoxicating scent. Relatively good repeat-bloomer. Growth sturdily upright, over 78 in. (200 cm) high; canes sturdy and furnished with many broad thorns. Foliage large, round, dark green. Use as impressive single planting, distance 101 in. (260 cm) apart. Also suitable as climbing rose on pillars or low walls. Also recommended: Its sport "Madame Ernst Calvat" with light rose flowers, also repeat-blooming.
My tip: Not entirely hardy in extreme winters. Recalls the mighty hybrid teas in its growth habit and the brilliance of its color.

Madame Boll

Zigeunerknabe
(= "Gypsy Boy")
Bourbon rose. Geschwind/ Lambert 1909.
Flowers dark lilac crimson to velvety dark violet with golden yellow stamens; medium-sized, $2^3/_4$ in. (7 cm) Ø, semidouble with 20 petals, rosette-shaped, usually in clusters; little scent; blooms once. Large, spherical, brilliant red hips. Growth extraordinarily vigorous, roundly bushy, quite well-branched, height over 98 in. (250 cm). Canes extremely thorny. Shrubs can fall apart somewhat. Foliage lush, large, dull green, coarse. Use as single planting in

Madame Isaac Pereire

Zigeunerknabe

larger gardens and parks, also possible as small climbing rose.

My tip: Frost-hardy. Tie up canes if necessary. Decorative hips.

Jacques Cartier

Portland rose. Moreau-Robert 1868.

Buds with long, sometimes feathery sepals. Flowers intense pink at first, then paler outsides in the sun; large-flowered, $3^1/_2$ in. (9 cm) Ø, very double with 30 petals lying loosely on top of each other, quartered; in the middle, the small petals are firmly turned inward in the "Damask button." This button formation is very common with very double Damask and Portland roses. Good scent. After a hiatus, abundant fall flowering starting in August. Self-cleaning down to the little "button." Growth upright, over 39 in. (100 cm) high; do not cut back in winter but only thin out to improve the shape. Foliage large, light-green, very dense, almost covering the buds. Use as single or group planting and for

Jacques Cartier

Charles Lawson

Madame Pierre Oger

hedges. Combines well with perennial neighbors. Problem-free care. Distance 59 in. (150 cm) apart.

Charles Lawson

Bourbon rose. Lawson 1853.

Buds large, rounded oval. Flowers pink-red; large, 4 in. (10 cm) Ø, very double with more than 30 petals, blooms only once, flowers usually slightly drooping. Lightly scented. Growth upright and strong, but falling apart. Develops beautiful, hanging flower clusters when the upright canes are supported in the center and held together; 78 in. (200 cm) high. Foliage fresh green, large, and loose, leaflets roundish. Use as single planting but good

with perennials to cover the bare lower bush; also use like a climbing rose on a column. Distance 86 in. (220 cm) apart.

My tip: Quite frost-hardy.

Madame Pierre Oger

Bourbon rose. Sport of "Reine Victoria." Oger/Verdier 1878.

Flowers light-suffused silvery mother-of-pearl pink, sometimes brushed with pale lilac on the outside, ivory in cooler weather; of symmetrical round shape, medium-sized, $2^3/_4$ in. (7 cm) Ø, graceful, loosely double, but never wholly open, blooming in clusters; pleasantly fragrant. Second flowering in late summer; vulnerable to rain. Growth slender with relatively thin canes, upright and overhanging, needs support. Height 59 in. (150 cm). Foliage pointed, dark green. Use this loosely growing shrub in hedges, also as single planting because of the charming flowers. Distance 70 in. (180 cm) apart, closer in hedges. The rose likes light shade and tolerates some draft. Also recommended: "Reine Victoria," deep old rose color to light red, better repeat-bloomer.

My tip: Suffers in extremely cold winters, susceptible to mildew and spot anthracnose. In close hedge plantings vulnerable to disease. Good soil and airy location help.

113

SHRUB ROSES

La Noblesse
Centifolia. Pastorel/Souper et Notting 1857.
Flowers transparent pink, darker in the center, medium-sized, 2 in. (6 cm) Ø, double, with 40 petals, quartered, good scent. Very late blooming, very susceptible to rain damage. Growth roundly bushy, 59 in. (150 cm) high, compact. Foliage dense, medium green, large. Use singly with low shrubs or in groups.

Rosa x centifolia "Muscosa"
(True) Moss rose. "Common Moss."
Sport of Rosa x centifolia.
Flowers pink, intense in the middle, like Rosa x centifolia or its "Cristata" form. Very dense and closed into an elongated dome shape, 4 in. (10 cm) Ø, double, over 60 delicate petals, vulnerable to rain damage. Balling is possible. Medium-length stems, somewhat drooping. The sepals on the roundish buds are filigreed with "moss" more than any other of the numerous moss rose varieties. These finely divided extensions begin on the stem with fine gland hairs, which increase in size toward the flower. The resinous scent of the moss lends a tart note to the heavy centifolia fragrance. Growth not so loosely spreading as Rosa x centifolia, rarely over 47 in. (120 cm) high. Foliage as with other centifolias, large, finely haired on underside or both sides, somewhat drooping. Use as shrub rose alone or in groups; distance 70 in. (180 cm). Also recommended: **"Muscosa Alba"** with white flowers. Rosa x centifolia "Andrewsii" is a "fallback" to a single, pink, wild rose flower with 5 petals and abundantly developed moss on stem and sepals. Important for breeding.

La Noblesse

My tip: Most beautiful and most widely distributed of the moss roses with incomparable fragrance. Unsprayed petals are the best ones for a rose punch.

Rosa x centifolia "Cristata"
"Chapeau de Napoléon." Variety of the cabbage rose or the Provence rose. Centifolia.
It has round buds, whose sepals sometimes have densely feathered leaf outgrowths on the edges, which look a bit like curly parsley, without glands; the calyx is smooth. Not a moss rose. The outgrowths form the figure of a "tricorn" over the closed bud, thus the name "Napoleon's hat"—especially charming with the just opening bud. Flowers silvery pure pink; large, 4 in. (10 cm) Ø, as a typical centifolia, the "hundred-petal rose," very densely double, over 60 delicate petals. Sweet-tart centifolia scent. Rain-damaged. Growth upright, outspreading, like almost all centifolias falls apart easily, up to 59 in. (150 cm) high. Foliage large; round leaflets of fresh, medium-

Muscosa Alba

Cristata

Fantin Latour

Marie de Blois

***Rosa* x *centifolia* "Major"**

few thorns. Foliage deep green, broad, glossy. Use as single planting or in small groups; too spreading for hedges. Distance 62 in. (160 cm) apart.

My tip: Light afternoon shade provided by shrubs that allow light through avoids fading in bright sunlight.

Marie de Blois
Moss rose. Robert 1852.
Flowers pure pink, later veiled with lilac; very large, $4^3/_4$ in. (12 cm) Ø, spherical and very double with 75 petals; marvelous "unfolding"; several in clusters; good fragrance. Growth somewhat more vigorous than "Muscosa," height 59 in. (150 cm); well-formed bushes. Canes with reddish moss bristles. Foliage large, fresh green. Use like all moss roses. Distance 70 in. (180 cm) apart.

My tip: There are many different colored moss roses, from white to dark violet red, but those in pink are the most beautiful.

Rosa x centifolia "Major"
(= "Cabbage Rose"), identical with "Rose des Peintres," cabbage rose, Provence rose.
18th century.
Flowers silvery pink; medium-sized, $2^3/_4$ in. (7 cm) Ø; spherical, very double; outstanding wild rose fragrance. Blooms once. Growth very overhanging, up to 78 in. (200 cm) high. Foliage medium green, dull. Use as single planting, also along a fence or in groups. Also recommended: "Ballata," the "lettuce rose" with large, vesicular puffy leaves.

My tip: *Rosa x centifolia* "Major" is also very attractive as a cut rose.

green color, matte. Use as single planting, also with perennials, which cover up the loose growth habit; also in groups.

Fantin Latour
A foundling of unknown origin ascribed to the centifolia group.
Flowers pale pink, darker in the middle; very classic, round, large saucer-shaped flowers of $3^1/_2$ in. (9 cm) Ø, which open into a cup shape and then expose the densely double, quartered center; over 50 petals. Wonderful scent. Growth sturdy, loosely branching, roundly bushy, up to 59 in. (150 cm) high,

SHRUB ROSES

William Allen Richardson
Noisette rose, sport of Rêve d'Or.
Ducher 1878.
<u>Flowers</u> amber-colored to apricot;
medium-sized, 2 in. (6 cm) Ø, double with 25 petals, good scent,
blooms heavily and repeatedly.
Large, round, red hips. <u>Growth</u> very
strong, forming stiff, broad, dense
bushes; 98 in. (250 cm) high. <u>Fo-
liage</u> large, dark green. <u>Use</u> as
climbing rose or as spreading
shrub by itself. Distance 137 in.
(350 cm) apart.
    My tip: Somewhat prone to
disease, but not so susceptible to
frost as it's reputed to be.

Hermosa
China rose. Marcheseau 1840.
<u>Flowers</u> pale lavender pink, trans-
parent; barely medium-sized, 2 in.
(5 cm) Ø, at first spherical, later
dish-shaped, quite double with 35
petals, but loose, sometimes quartered; always growing in bunches;
delicate fragrance. With noticeable
hiatus, reblooms well until fall.
<u>Growth</u> moderate, delicate, thin-
caned, upright, well-branched, 35
in. (90 cm) high. <u>Foliage</u> dainty,
bluish green, lush. <u>Use</u> in mixed
borders, also as filler, in corners in
front of higher bushes or in small
groups. As a lone plant in summer,
somewhat "diaphanous." Distance
39 in. (100 cm) apart. <u>Also recommended:</u> Its climbing sport "<u>Setina</u>"
in the same coloring.
    My tip: Moderately disease-
prone and, for a China rose, astonishingly winter-hardy. Nevertheless, winter protection against
frost recommended. Prune like
repeat-flowering shrub roses.

William Allen Richardson

Hermosa

Old Blush

Stanwell Perpetual

Old Blush
(= "Parsons Pink China")
China rose, shrub rose. From
China, cultivated in England since
1713.
<u>Flowers</u> pale pink at first, then dark-
ening; medium-sized, 2³/₄ in. (7
cm) Ø, semidouble with 20 petals,
blooming in large clusters; little
scent. Somewhat repeating, after a

definite hiatus. <u>Growth</u> moderately
strong, overhanging, rather thin-
caned, height 39 in. (100 cm). <u>Fo-
liage</u> medium-green, medium-sized,
leaflets pointed oval with extended
tips. <u>Use</u> as bedding and shrub
rose. Distance 55 in. (140 cm)
apart. <u>Also recommended:</u> More robust and truly ever-blooming until
fall but not so graceful is "<u>Bengal
Crimson</u>"; it is rose red and single,
with 5 petals.
    My tip: Susceptible to leaf dis-
eases. Winter protection is recommended. Ancient cultivated rose of
great charm, interesting plant for
rose lovers.

116

Gloire de Dijon

Rosa chinensis "Viridiflora"

Stanwell Perpetual

Pimpinellifolia x Damask Rose. Lee 1838.

<u>Flowers</u> light pale pink to white; medium-sized, 2 in. (6 cm) Ø; densely double, very shallow, with "Damask button," occurring singly or several together; good fragrance. Very lush bloomer, full bloom beginning of June, but almost never without at least one flower until frost. <u>Growth</u> medium strong. Forms beautiful, densely compact, round bushes, 59 in. (150 cm) high and wide. <u>Foliage</u> gray-green, with 5–7 small round leaflets. <u>Use</u> as single planting in a heather garden or with other Pimpinellifolia roses. Also suitable as a dense, tall bedding rose. Distance 66 in. (170 cm) apart.

My tip: Probably the least problematic nostalgic rose for the beginner. Also an interesting dwarfed rose on a standard.

Gloire de Dijon

Noisette or tea rose. Climbing rose. Jacotot 1853.

<u>Flowers</u> light orange yellow, creamy white on outside, with orange and pink hues; large-flowered, 4 in. (10 cm) Ø, densely double with 35 petals, quartered effect, short-stemmed, and early blooming. Strong fragrance. Sometimes flowers nod a little. Reblooms well, with short or longer intervals depending on exposure, right up until frost. <u>Growth</u> is strong, up to 195 in. (500 cm) high. <u>Foliage</u> medium-sized, often somewhat sparse. <u>Use</u> for walls, pillars.

My tip: Astonishingly winter-hardy. The only tea rose that can be recommended as an experiment in nostalgia because of its hardiness and vigor, although it is prone to spot anthracnose and red spider. Difficult in light, sandy soils. Try summer pruning after first flowering. Fertilize heavily with organic fertilizer. Western exposure appears to be favorable.

Rosa chinensis "Viridiflora"

Green Rose.
Cluster-flowered rose. Known since 1833 (USA).

<u>Flowers</u> with very numerous, completely green, very small petals with a sawtoothed edge, which must be described as bracts because of their form and color; small, 2 in. (5 cm) Ø; keep for a very long time and fade to bronze purple. Completely sterile. Blooms in large clusters, rarely singly. <u>Growth</u> bushy like a floribunda rose, 23 in. (60 cm) high. <u>Foliage</u> medium-green, pointed oval leaflets. <u>Use</u> as a curiosity for garden and vase.

My tip: Healthy for the most part but is attacked by spider mites.

SHRUB ROSES

Mrs. John Laing
Hybrid Perpetual. Bennet 1887.
<u>Flowers</u> pure rose; large, 4 in. (11 cm) Ø, quite double, with 35 petals, but loose, at first spherical, later bowl-shaped; quite rainfast because of thick petals and keeps well; usually in clusters of 3–5 flowers. Strong, pleasing scent. <u>Growth</u> sturdy, broadly bushy, but can sprawl. Canes thin. Only prickles instead of thorns. <u>Foliage</u> fresh, light green, dense. <u>Use</u> best as single planting. Will fit well into hedges and beds, however. Distance 59 in. (150 cm) apart.
　　My tip: Outstanding hybrid perpetual for beginners.

Ferdinand Pichard
Hybrid Perpetual. π Tanne 1921.
<u>Buds</u> large, round-oval. <u>Flowers</u> red to scarlet and pink-striped on a white ground; large, 4 in. (11 cm) Ø; very double with 30 petals; usually 3–5 flowers per stem; strong fragrance. <u>Growth</u> strong, 47 in. (120 cm) high. <u>Foliage</u> dark green, light green at first. <u>Use</u> for groups. Combination with other plants is difficult because of the tricky color.
　　My tip: Anyone who especially likes striped flowers will enjoy this variety.

Roger Lambelin
Hybrid Perpetual. Vve. Schwartz 1890. Sport of "Fisher and Holmes."
<u>Flowers</u> intense crimson purple with brownish violet background, narrowly white-edged and slightly striped; large, 4 in. (10 cm) Ø, edge wavy almost like a carnation, very double with over 40 petals; fragrant; repeat-bloomer. <u>Growth</u> sturdy, thickly branching, 55 in. (140 cm) high. <u>Foliage</u> large, medium-green, matte, covers well. <u>Use</u> best as a

Mrs. John Laing

single planting or in groups with other old roses. Distance 59 in. (150 cm) apart. <u>Also recommended:</u> Similar dark crimson red but not so wavy is "<u>Reine des Violettes</u>,"

Miller Mallet 1869, with medium-sized flowers; smells like lilacs; very good as a single planting or in a mixed bed.

Ferdinand Pichard

Heinrich Conrad Söth

Roger Lambelin

Penelope

Felicia

Heinrich Conrad Söth

Lambertiana rose. Lambert 1919.
Flowers brilliant rose red with almost white eye; small, $^3/_4$ in. (2 cm) Ø, single with 5 petals; in cone-shaped panicles of many, like phlox, situated at the ends of sturdy canes; good fragrance. Repeats well. Growth sturdy with slender canes, which hang down, widely spreading shrub. Foliage medium-sized, dark green, glossy. Use preferably as a repeat-blooming shrub rose in groups or in a mixed border, goes well with perennials. Distance 59 in. (150 cm) apart. Also recommended: This historically interesting and also very beautiful variety is an early forerunner of quite similar varieties, as, for example, "Mozart" (Lambert 1937), "Ballerina" (Bentall 1937), and "Robin Hood" (Pemberton 1927), which are classified as hybrid musk roses. All rebloom abundantly. They are still widely available today and are worth recommending for their somewhat different color nuances.

My tip: It is worth noting that this small-flowered rose is fragrant.

Felicia

Hybrid Musk, shrub rose. Pemberton 1928.
Flowers pastel salmon pink with shading, later somewhat paler to almost white; medium-sized, $3^1/_2$ in. (9 cm) Ø, loosely double with 30 petals, shallow; outstanding fragrance. Flowers lushly and repeatedly in clusters at the ends of canes. Growth moderately strong, very densely branching, 59 in. (150 cm) high. Foliage thick, dark green, matte. Use alone or in groups in mixed plantings. Distance 70 in. (180 cm) apart. Also recommended:

"Cornelia," 1925, salmon pink with apricot, small-flowered, semidouble; "Buff Beauty," Bentall 1939, amber to apricot, very double, large-flowered in bunches; "Penelope," 1924, cream-colored with pink, fading to almost white; semidouble; "Danaë," 1913, golden yellow to cream, vigorously growing; "Daybreak," 1918, yellow; "Pax," 1918, pure white, semidouble; and "Prosperity," 1919, with creamy white, large, double flowers. The pastel shades of the colors are typical for these varieties. The variety "Moonlight," 1913, has only medium-sized, single, creamy white flowers with only 5–10 petals and very beautiful golden yellow stamens. Almost all these varieties are roses from the grower J. Pemberton, who has slipped into undeserved oblivion. Not from Pemberton is the completely problem-free musk rose "Narrow Water" (Daisy Hill Nurseries 1883) with semidouble silvery to lavender pink saucer-shaped flowers that have a very pleasant scent.

My tip: "Felicia" is a very free-flowering, delightful shrub rose without any problems for the beginner and the experienced alike. The form of the shrub can be corrected through pruning as desired, and it goes well with both bushes and shrubs.

SHRUB ROSES

Wife of Bath
Austin 1969.
Flowers pure rose, darker at the center; large at over 4 in. (11 cm) Ø at first round, very double with 40 petals, developing like old roses, tangy fragrance. Flowers occur singly or several together on last year's wood, but also on new growth, continuously flowering. Growth dense, bushy, robust, 35 in. (90 cm) high. Foliage medium green, not very large, coarse veins. Use like old roses or shrub roses in groups or singly, also in combination with perennials, distance 47 in. (120 cm) apart. Because of its lower growth habit, this shrub rose may be used as a bedding rose as well.

The Prioress
Austin 1969.
Flowers pale pink with some salmon color; round to cup-shaped, medium-sized at 3 $\frac{1}{2}$ in. (9 cm) Ø, semidouble with 20 petals, clearly visible stamens, continuous blooming; delicate fragrance. Growth sturdy, 49 in. (125 cm) high. Foliage medium green, leathery. Use for group and single plantings. Distance 55 in. (140 cm) apart.

The Miller
Austin 1970
Flowers pure rose, pale pink outside, inside darker, transparent; good medium size, 3 $\frac{1}{2}$ in. (9 cm) Ø, cup-shaped at first, then flattening, loosely double with 25 petals, growing singly or in clusters, hanging and nodding, continuous flowering; good fragrance. Growth strong, 59 to 70 in. (150–180 cm) high. Foliage deep green. Use for hedges, groups, and singly. Can be combined well with perennials. Distance 70 in. (180 cm) apart.

Wife of Bath

The Prioress

The Miller

Chianti

My tip: Better flowering with pruning.

Chianti
Austin 1967.
Flowers deep wine red; medium-sized, 3 in. (8 cm) Ø, semidouble with 28 petals, urn-shaped; attractive golden yellow stamens; flowers in clusters, once-blooming, fragrant. Growth strong, 59 in. (150 cm) high. Foliage dark green, semi-glossy. Use singly or in groups. Also recommended: Similar in color but more crimson and more double are "Vivid" and "Fisherman's Friend," both easy to care for and continuously blooming.

English Roses

Lilian Austin

Constance Spry

Charles Austin

Constance Spry
Austin/Sunningdale 1961.
Flowers pure pink; very large, $4^3/_4$ in. (12 cm) Ø, round at first, quite double with 30 petals; flowers lined up along the branches, once-blooming; sweetly scented. Growth sturdy, 68–78 in. (175–200 cm) high, quite thorny. Foliage luxuriant, medium-sized, leathery, gray green, reddish when new. Use for groups or alone, also very beautiful for pillars of 78 in. (200 cm). Goes well with perennials. Also recommended: "Heritage," Austin 1984, pure pink, lighter at edges, 3 in. (8 cm) Ø, very doubled and quartered; lushly flowering until frost; fragrant. Adequately rainfast. 47 in. (120 cm) high.
   My tip: A rose for which you willingly take its one-time flowering in stride because of its beauty.

Charles Austin
Austin 1973.
Flowers light orange with yellow; very large, $4^3/_4$ in. (12 cm) Ø, "old-fashioned" quartering, extremely double with 40 petals, urn-shaped, luxuriantly flowering, one second flowering; strongly scented. Growth strong, bushy, upright, 59 in. (150 cm) high. Foliage large, light green, glossy. Use alone or in groups. Distance 62 in. (160 cm) apart.
   My tip: Combine its pastel-shaded play of color with pale blue and lavender perennials.

Lilian Austin
David Austin 1973.
Flowers strongly salmon-colored, going to apricot to orange at the center; large, 4–$4^3/_4$ in. (10–12 cm) Ø, rosette form; growing in clusters; fragrant. Continuously flowering. Growth branching, arching, and overhanging, 49 in. (125 cm) high. Foliage medium-sized, dark green, faintly glossy. Use as single planting or in groups.
   My tip: The pastel play of colors in this and most of the other English roses is something new for the use of roses in the garden. It would pay to experiment.

121

SHRUB ROSES

Variety	Grower/Year	Flower	Height in in. (cm)	Comments
Modern Varieties				
Blossomtime	O'Neal/ Bosley 1951	dark pink, 4¼ in. (11 cm) Ø, densely double, repeat-bloomer	66 (170)	Marvelous scent; romantic rose; problems: rain, mildew, spot anthracnose.
Burghausen	Kordes 1991	bloodred, 3 in. (8 cm) Ø, loosely double, repeats	78 (200)	ADR rose 1989; thick canes.
Canary Bird	unknown	canary yellow, 2¾ in. (7 cm) Ø, single, blooms once	59 (150)	Hybrid of *Rosa hugonis* x *Rosa xanthina*, very early; good scent.
Frühlingsgold	Kordes 1937	golden yellow, 4 in. (10 cm) Ø, single, blooms once	98 (250)	Comes from *Rosa pimpinellifolia*, very early, a little repeat flowering.
Golden Wings	Shephard/ Bosley 1956	yellow, 4¼ in. (11 cm) Ø, single, repeat-bloomer	59 (150)	Large orange red stamens.
Royal Show	Meilland 1983	dark red, 3 in. (8 cm) Ø, loosely double, repeat-bloomer	78 (200)	Healthy; also use as as small climbing rose.
Vogelpark Walsrode	Kordes 1988	light pink, 3½ in. (9 cm) Ø, loosely double repeat-bloomer	59 (150)	ADR Rose 1982; healthy extended flowering, eye-catcher.
Old Roses and Historic Varieties				
Baron Girod de l'Ain	Reverchon 1897	violet red, 3 in. (8 cm) Ø, very double, repeat-bloomer	47 (120)	Hybrid Perpetual. Wavy petals with white edge, fragrant.
Bourbon Queen	Bréon/Mauget 1835	crimson pink, 3 in. (8 cm) Ø, very double, blooms once	117 (300)	Bourbon rose. Strong scent, heavy flowering.
Fritz Nobis	Kordes 1940	white/pink, 3½ in. (9 cm) Ø, semidouble, blooms once	78 (200)	*Rubiginosa* hybrid. Strong fragrance, flowers luxuriantly.
Général Jacqueminot	Roussel 1853	velvet red, 4 in. (10 cm) Ø, double, repeat-bloomer	47 (120)	Hybrid Perpetual. Strong fragrance, bushy.
Général Kléber	Robert 1856	mother-of-pearl pink, 2¼ in. (6 cm) Ø, densely double, blooms once	59 (150)	Moss rose. Pleasing overhanging growth habit, some scent.
Hebe's Lip	Paul 1912	creamy white with pink edge, 3 in. (8 cm) Ø, semi-double, blooms once	59 (150)	*Rubiginosa* hybrid. Musk scent.
Königin von Dänemark	Booth 1816	crimson pink, 3 in. (8 cm) Ø, double, blooms once, quartered	51 (130)	*Rosa alba.* Vulnerable to rain, healthy foliage, fragrant.
La Reine Victoria	Schwartz 1872	silky pink, 4 in. (10 cm) Ø, double, repeat-bloomer	59 (150)	Bourbon rose. Loves airy location and good soil.
Louise Odier	Margottin 1851	light pinkish red, 2 in. (5 cm) Ø, very densely doubled, repeat-bloomer	62 (160)	Bourbon rose. Lasting, perfectly formed flowers, also keep when cut.

Variety	Grower/Year	Flower	Height in in. (cm)	Comments
Maiden's Blush	15th century	pale pink, 3½ in. (9 cm) Ø, double, blooms once	78 (200)	*Rosa alba.* Scent delicious, little sensitivity.
Malvina	Verdier 1841	light pink, 2¼ in. (6 cm) Ø, very double, repeat-bloomer	39 (100)	Moss rose. Fragrant, beautiful moss; large, healthy, resembles "Salet."
Mme Hardy	Hardy 1832	snow white, 2¾ in. (7 cm) Ø, double, blooms once	59 (150)	*Rosa x damascena.* Blooms heavily, delicately scented, green eye, healthy.
Mm Plantier	Plantier 1835	cream, then white, 2¾ in. (7 cm) Ø, very double, blooms once	66 (170)	*Rosa alba.* Easy care and winter-hardy, almost thornless, good for creeping or climbing.
Parfum de l'Haÿ	Gravereaux 1901	crimson, 3 in. (8 cm) Ø, double, repeats	59 (150)	*Rugosa* hybrid. Drooping flowers, fragrant, later flowering meager.
Parvifolia (Rose de Meaux)		dark rose, 1 in. (3 cm) Ø, double, blooms once	20 (50)	Small centifolia. "Burgundy rose," early, for small gardens.
Pink Grootendorst	Grootendorst 1923	soft pink, 1½ in. (4 cm) Ø, double, blooms once	47 (120)	*Rugosa* hybrid. Carnation rose. Sport of "F. J. Grootendorst" (red).
Schneezwerg	Lambert 1912	white, 1½ in. (4 cm) Ø, semidouble, repeats	59 (150)	Rugosa hybrid. Yellow stamens, in fall flowers and fruits at the same time.
Semiplena	13th century	white, 2¾ in. (7 cm) Ø, semidouble, blooms once	78 (200)	*Rosa alba.* White peony, long blooming period, scented, prone to rust.
Souvenir de la Malmaison	Béluze 1843	cream white, 4 in. (10 cm) Ø, double, repeats	23 (60)	Bourbon rose. Quartered, extremely fragrant, for the small garden.
Tuscany Superb	before 1845	dark red, 4 in. (10 cm) Ø, double, blooms once	59 (150)	*Rosa gallica.* Brownish shadings with velvety spots.
Ulrich Brunner Fils	A. Levet 1882	cherry red, 3½ in. (9 cm) Ø, double, repeats	35 (90)	Hybrid Perpetual. Good scent, healthy, for beginners also.

English Roses

Variety	Grower/Year	Flower	Height in in. (cm)	Comments
Abraham Darby	Austin 1985	apricot yellow with pink, 4 in. (10 cm) Ø, double, repeats	59–82 (150–210)	Strong fragrance, very healthy.
Chaucer	Austin 1970	subdued deep pink, 4¾ in. (12 cm) Ø, double, repeats	39 (100)	Similarity to Gallicas, tangy fragrance.
Glastonbury	Austin 1974	deep red, 4 in. (10 cm) Ø, double, repeats	59 (150)	Yellow stamens, strong centifolia fragrance.
Graham Thomas	Austin 1983	amber, 3 in. (8 cm) Ø, double, repeats	59 (150)	Sturdy, upright growth.
Heritage	Austin 1984	pure pink, 3 in. (8 cm) Ø, densely double, repeats	47 (120)	Luxuriant flowering, sufficiently rainfast.

GROUND-COVERING ROSES

These roses are supposed to cover the ground so thickly that weeds can't even get started. They need not be only the creeping, close-lying varieties. Various higher-growing roses may be classed in this group, so long as their foliage is dense enough to deny weeds light.

Background
Even around the turn of the century, thus long before they were called "ground-covering roses," thin-caned, creeping roses were allowed to ramble over the ground to create splendidly blooming embankments.

In the middle '70s, blooming roses were tried out on public open spaces as "a cheerful ground cover." Great success resulted with low-lying, soft-caned climbing roses like "Max Graf" or extremely wide-growing, thickly branching shrub roses like *Rosa rugosa* "Dagmar Hastrup."

Roses used for ground covering should not be prone to pests or disease, should be easy to care for, and should be everblooming. Crossing has now created higher-growing varieties that, being shrub roses, enrich the selection, like "Smarty," "Snow Ballet," and "The Fairy." Recently there have also been everblooming ground-covering roses bred from the cluster-flowered bedding and shrub roses.

Working with Ground Covers
Many of these roses are charming, luxuriantly flowering small shrubs and are very healthy. As partners of shrubs and perennials, they have become an important rose class for small gardens. Beyond that they are used in very different ways, depending on their growth habits.

• You can let low-growing ground covers ripple over walls or down steps.

• Ground covers are excellent roses for natural front yards.

• There are now many ever-blooming varieties that can be used like shrub roses.

Classification of Growth Habits

Nurseries haven't yet been able to agree on a single system. I content myself here with these four groups:

1. flatly recumbent;
2. stiff, broadly upright;
3. spreading and shrubby;
4. archingly overhanging, upright.

The following descriptions of varieties refer to these growth groups.

The ground-cover rose "Fairy Red" is one of the many daughters of "The Fairy." Here it is seen together with *Aster amellus* "Dr. Otto Petschek."

GROUND-COVERING ROSES

Palmengarten Frankfurt
Shrub rose/ground-cover rose.
Kordes 1988, ADR Rose 1992.
<u>Buds</u> very small, round with a slight point, in many-flowered clusters. <u>Flowers</u> intense dark crimson pink, almost light red; medium-sized, 2 in. (6 cm) Ø, loosely doubled with 16 petals, little scent; very heavy bloomer, self-cleaning. <u>Growth</u> broadly spreading to overhanging, only up to 35 in. (90 cm) high. Good continued growth. Growth types 3–4. <u>Foliage</u> fresh medium green with high gloss. Good background for flowers. <u>Use</u> as ground cover, also alone or with other shrubs, 43 in. (110 cm) apart or one plant per 11 sq ft (1 sq m).

My tip: Very healthy, easily cultured, and attractive.

Heidekönigin
Climbing rose/ground-cover rose.
Kordes 1985.
<u>Buds</u> small, spherical, on clusters at the ends of canes. <u>Flowers</u> pure pink with a play of color in the sun; 2 in. (6 cm) Ø, 20 transparent petals, loose, but well-doubled, round. Some fragrance. Very late unfolding of flowers; keeps well, even with rain; blooms once, self-cleaning. <u>Growth</u> like a soft-caned climbing rose (rambler type), canes over 117 in. (300 cm) long, lying close to the ground. Growth type 1. <u>Foliage</u> small to medium-sized, dense, fresh green, glossy. <u>Use</u> for embankments; 47 in. (120 cm) apart or 1 plant every 16 sq ft (1.5 sq m); as climbing rose on pergolas; also as cascade rose. <u>Also recommended:</u> "<u>Immensee</u>" and "<u>Repandia</u>," brilliant pink (ADR Rose), both also in white. Similar growth habits.

My tip: Very healthy. The late flowering renders many flowers

Palmengarten Frankfurt

when other roses are getting ready for their second blooming.

The Fairy
Polyantha/ground-cover rose.
Bentall 1932.
<u>Buds</u> small, spherical, pink. <u>Flowers</u> light pink, in large, many-flowered, ball-shaped clusters, which burst forth just at the end of June; slightly fading when in full bloom; $^{3}/_{4}$–1 in. (2–2.5 cm) Ø, densely double, like pompoms; little scent. Not entirely rainfast, not self-cleaning, but blooms luxuriantly and repeatedly until frost. <u>Growth</u> medium sturdy, with soft spreading or overhanging light green canes; very densely branching, thus in spite of small,

Heidekönigin

slender leaves, provides good cover; growth type 3. <u>Foliage</u> light green at first, later medium green. <u>Use</u> as bedding rose or spread flat, charming on banks. Distance 16 in. (40 cm) apart. Also good as small shrub rose; then put them farther apart.

The Fairy

Snow Ballet

Mirato

Rosy Carpet

Also recommended: Of the same variety as "The Fairy," "Fairy Dance," bloodred, and "Fairyland," light pink, are particularly interesting.

My tip: In summer some mildew; usually in October spot anthracnose. Good also as standard and semistandard rose. Fills the blooming gap left by the first flowering of the floribunda roses. Anyone who prefers white to pink can arrive at a similar effect with the very good "Alba Meidiland."

Snow Ballet
Shrub rose/ground-cover rose. Clayworth 1978.
Buds globe-shaped, creamy white. Flowers pure white, at first yellowish pink in the center; medium-sized, 2 in. (5–6 cm) Ø; densely doubled, 40–60 petals, growing alone or in short-stemmed clusters; weak scent. Very abundant second flowering, not self-cleaning; forms balls with rain. Growth branching, archingly overhanging. Canes thin. Forms dense, round bushes and good ground cover of 23 in. (60 cm) in height; growth type 3. Fo-

liage just barely medium-sized, with seven leaflets, dense, dark green, and glossy. Use as a good ground cover for flat expanses, groupings, wide enclosures. Distance 23 in. (60 cm) apart or three plants every 11 sq ft (1 sq m). When planted alone, give it 39 in. (100 cm) to spread.

My tip: Healthy, somewhat mildew-prone in late summer. Cut off the faded flowers as much as possible.

Mirato
Shrub rose/ground-cover rose. Tantau 1990.
Buds round, fat. Flowers glowing pink; medium-sized, 2 in. (5 cm) Ø; slightly doubled, growing in broad clusters; no scent. Very luxuriant, but blooms only once. Growth bushy, broad, $15\frac{1}{2}$ in. (40 cm) high. Growth type 3. Foliage round, medium green, glossy. Use for wide-area ground cover and front yards; for greening embankments. Plant 20 in. (50 cm) apart, four plants per 11 sq ft (1 sq m).

Rosy Carpet
Shrub rose/ground-cover rose. Interplant 1984.
Buds markedly pointed cones, medium-sized. Flowers crimson pink with small, yellow stamens; small, 2 in. (5 cm) Ø, single, 5–7 slightly wavy petals; in lush clusters; wild rose fragrance. Everblooming. Growth very bushy and spreading, good continued growth, 31 in. (80 cm) high. Growth type 4. Foliage medium-sized, dark green, glossy, dense. Use for area plantings, embankments, 3 plants per 11 sq ft (1 sq m), distance 23 in. (60 cm) apart.

My tip: Complements the delicate rose pink "Roseromantic" well. Somewhat prone to mildew, otherwise robust.

127

GROUND-COVERING ROSES

Red Yesterday
(= "Marjorie Fair")
Shrub rose. Harkness 1978,
ADR Rose 1980.
Buds small, cherry red; numerous
buds grow in a ball-shaped or elongated cluster. Flowers a brilliant dark
red with white centers; small, $3/4$ to 1
in. (2–3 cm) Ø, single, 5 petals; no
scent. Growth as shrub rose moderately vigorous, partly upright, partly
loosely trailing to outspreading, 31
in. (80 cm) high. Growth type 3. Foliage small, elongated; copper-col-
ored when new, then a glossy light
green, loose but nevertheless covering. Use well as isolated group of
three, also as area planting. When
covering embankments use 3–4
plants every 11 sq ft (1 sq m),
spaced 23 in. (60 cm) apart.

Pink Meidiland
Shrub rose/ground-cover rose.
Meilland 1984.
Buds pointed oval, crimson red.
Flowers at first intense salmon with
white eye and golden yellow stamens, later lightening; medium-
sized 2 in. (5–6 cm) Ø, single,
usually 5 petals; continuous
bloomer, self-cleaning. Growth
sturdy, upright, bushy, densely
branching, 35 in. (90 cm) high.
Growth type 2–3. Foliage good
medium size, dark green. Use as
good ground cover and as bedding
rose of floribunda type.

Ballerina
Shrub rose/ground-cover rose.
Bentall 1937.
Buds small, round, oval. Flowers
pale pink with white eye; single,
small-flowered, $3/4$ in. (2 cm) Ø, but
abundantly flowering in many large
clusters; little scent. Continues to
bloom well all summer long.
Growth spreading, archingly over-

Red Yesterday

hanging; 39–59 in. (100–150 cm)
high. Growth type 3. Foliage light
green, small, coarse, lush. Use for
single or group plantings, also horizontally as a high ground cover for
banks; good in combination with
perennials. Plant two to every 11 sq
ft (1 sq m). When using alone,
allow 39 in. (100 cm) space.

My tip: Easy-care variety with
continuous blooming; also striking
as a standard. To promote reflowering, remove faded clusters and prevent formation of hips.

Pink Meidiland

Heidi

Ballerina

Lavender Dream

Heidi
Shrub rose, ground-cover rose. Noack 1987.
Buds small and pointed in large clusters. Flowers intense pink, usually with lighter spots along the petal edges; 2 in. (5 cm) Ø; the petals are turned and wavy, beautiful yellow stamens in the simple saucer flower, self-cleaning. Growth strong, bushily branched, growth type 2, some 27 in. (70 cm) tall, continues to make new growth. Foliage large, medium green to dark green, some gloss, dense. Use as ground-cover rose at distances of 23 in. (60 cm) or three plants per 11 sq ft (1 sq m), but also good as a small shrub or bedding or border rose. Also recommended: "Heidetraum," strong pink, and "Wildfang," brilliant pink, both ADR Roses of 1990 and 1991.

Lavender Dream
Shrub rose/ground-cover rose. Interplant 1985, ADR Rose 1987.
Buds small, in large clusters.

Moje Hammarberg

Flowers lavender blue; $1^1/_2$ in. (4 cm) Ø; single saucer-shaped flower, 5–8 petals, keeps very well, resists rain damage, self-cleaning; fragrant; blooms heavily and often. Growth loose, branching, weak-caned, archingly overhanging to recumbent. Growth type 3. Height 23 in. (60 cm). Foliage medium-sized, glossy. Use as a very good ground cover for banks and walls. Distance 31 in. (80 cm) apart or 1–2 plants every 11 sq ft (1 sq m). Very good together with perennials.
　My tip: Easy culture.

Moje Hammarberg
Shrub rose/ground-cover rose. Hammarberg 1931, seedling of *Rosa rugosa*.
Buds elongated with long sepals, a few in small clusters. Flowers lilac red; $3^1/_2$ in. (9 cm) Ø, semidouble, 20 petals, on very short, often nodding stems. Stamens golden yellow; intense fragrance. Heavy flowering mid-June, reblooming at beginning of September. Large, flattened-globular, red hips up to 1 in. (2.5 cm) Ø. Growth stiff, bushy, twiggy, densely branched, 39 in. (100 cm) high. Growth type 3. Canes very thorny. Foliage dark green, wrinkled, leathery, dense. Use 31 in. (80 cm) apart or two plants per 11 sq ft (1 sq m) for area planting, banks, or in groups. Also recommended: "Dagmar Hastrup," pink, single, saucer-shaped flower, 27 in. (70 cm) high; "Smarty," white, with apricot, 47 in. (120 cm) high. Some less mildew-prone varieties: "Fair Play," bright red, violet shadings, semidouble, 59 in. (150 cm) high; "Fiona," blood red to dark crimson, loosely doubled, 35 in. (90 cm) high; "Rosy Cushion," light pink, single, up to 47 in. (120 cm) high; "Fleurette," pink, small-flowered, single, up to 47 in. (120 cm) high; "Candy Rose," crimson with white eye, 27 in. (70 cm) high; "Rush," white inside, pink outside, single, 55 in. (140 cm) high, very good; "IGA '83 München" (ADR Rose 1982), crimson pink, semidouble, 47 in. (120 cm) high; "Rokoko," cream-colored, semidouble, 55 in. (140 cm) high; "Sea Foam," white, double, 39 in. (100 cm) high.
　My tip: "Moje Hammarberg" is salt-tolerant, completely frost-hardy, but on lime-rich soil it is prone to chlorosis.

GROUND-COVERING ROSES

Variety	Grower/Year	Flower	Growth type 1–4	No. Plants*	Comments

Recumbent Varieties

Variety	Grower/Year	Flower	Growth type 1–4	No. Plants*	Comments
Alba Meidiland	Strobel 1987	white, 1 in. (3 cm) Ø, double, repeat-blooming	3–4	1	Very healthy, not entirely rainfast; cut off balled flowers.
Apfelblüte	Noack 1982	light pink, 1½ in. (4 cm) Ø, semidouble, repeat-blooming	3	1	ADR Rose 1991, very healthy, little care.
Candy Rose	Meilland 1990	salmon light pink, 2 in. (5 cm) Ø, semidouble, repeat-blooming	3	3	Broadly bushy.
Heidetraum	Noack 1988	rose red, 1½ in. (4 cm) Ø, semidouble, repeat-blooming	3	2	ADR Rose 1990, very healthy.
Immensee	Kordes 1982	mother-of-pearl pink, 1 in. (3 cm) Ø, single, blooms once	1	1	Very healthy, green in winter, little care, good fragrance.
Kent	Poulsen 1991	white, 1½ in. (4 cm) Ø, semidouble, repeat-blooming	3	3	Small, flowers have beautiful stamens.
Mainaufeuer	Kordes 1990	dark red, 2 in. (5 cm) Ø, double, repeat-blooming	4	2	Noticeable stamens.
Max Graf	Bowditch 1919	light pink, 2 in. (5 cm) Ø, single, blooms once	1	1	Also a rambler, sturdy, thorny.
Heideröslein Nozomi	Onodera 1968	light pink, ¾ in. (2 cm) Ø, single, blooms once	1	2	Reblooms only slightly.
Pink Spray	Lens 1980	pink, 1 in. (3 cm) Ø, single, blooms once	3	1	Long- but not quite repeat-blooming; similarly "White Spray," white.
Pearl Meidiland	Meilland	pastel pink, 1½ in. (4 cm) Ø, double, repeat-blooming	1	3	Similar varieties: "Scarlet Meidiland" (scarlet), "Red Meidiland" (red).
Repandia	Kordes 1982	pink, 1 in. (3 cm) Ø, single, blooms once	1	1	Also as rambler, very healthy, evergreen.
Red Max Graf	Kordes 1980	bloodred, 2 in. (5 cm) Ø, single, blooms once	1	1	Forms thickets.
White Immensee	Kordes 1982	white, 1 in. (3 cm) Ø, single, blooms once	1	1	Also a rambler, very healthy, evergreen.
White Repandia	Kordes 1982	white, 1 in. (3 cm) Ø, single, blooms once	1	1	Lightly scented, very healthy, also a rambler, evergreen.
Wildfang	Noack 1989	pink, 1½ in. (4 cm) Ø, semidouble, repeat-blooming	3	1	ADR Rose 1991, very healthy, evergreen.

*Indicates number of plants that should be planted in an 11 square foot (square meter) area.

Variety	Grower/Year	Flower	Growth type 1–4	No. Plants*	Comments

Higher-growing Varieties

Variety	Grower/Year	Flower	Growth type 1–4	No. Plants*	Comments
Fair Play	Interplant 1978	bright red, 2 in. (5 cm) Ø, semidouble, repeat-blooming	4	2	Yellow stamens, loose, overhanging growth.
Ferdy	Keisei 1984	red with yellow, 1½ in. (4 cm) Ø, semidouble, once-blooming	3	2	Luxuriant flowers, healthy.
Fiona	Meilland 1979	bloodred, 1½ in. (4 cm) Ø, double, repeat-blooming	4	2	Somewhat mildew-prone.
Fleurette	Interplant 1978	crimson pink, 2 in. (5 cm) Ø, semidouble, repeat-blooming	4	2	Upright, overhanging growth, somewhat mildew-prone.
IGA '83 München	Meilland 1982	crimson pink, 3 in. (8 cm) Ø, semidouble, repeat-blooming	3	1	ADR Rose 1982, also good as bedding rose. Decorative hips.
Marondo	Kordes 1991	strong pink, 2 in. (5 cm) Ø, semidouble, once-blooming	1	3	ADR Rose 1989.
Red Bells	Olesen/ Poulsen 1980	red, 1½ in. (4 cm) Ø, double, blooms once	1–3	3	Flowers often hidden, older plants more beautiful.
Romanze	Tantau 1984	intense pink, 4 in. (10 cm) Ø, loosely double, once-blooming	4	2	ADR Rose 1986, good with perennials, also alone.
Rosa rugosa "Monte Cassino"	Baum 1987	crimson red, 2¼ in. (6 cm) Ø, double, repeat-blooming	2	3	One of the countless rugosa varieties such as "Dagmar Hastrup," "Rosa Zwerg," "Pieretta" (ADR 1992), "Polareis," "Rotes Meer."
Rosy Cushion	Interplant 1981	light pink, 2 in. (5 cm) Ø, single, repeat-blooming	4	2	Always blooms in clusters, light green foliage.
Rote Woge	Meilland/ Strobel 1991	dark red, 2¼ in. (6 cm) Ø, double, repeat-blooming	3	3	Also suitable as healthy bedding rose or small shrub.
Rush	Lens 1983	pink, white center, 1½ in. (4 cm) Ø, single, repeat-blooming	4	2	Interesting hybrid of *Rosa multiflora adenochaeta*.
White Hedge	unknown	white, 2¾ in. (7 cm) Ø, single, repeat-blooming	3	3	*Rugosa* foliage but no scent.

*Indicates number of plants that should be planted in an 11 square foot (square meter) area.

Portraits
BEDDING ROSES

I n the following portraits you will learn about hybrid teas, floribundas, and miniature roses.

Large-flowered Hybrid Teas
The hybrid teas have decorated the rose scene for about a hundred years. Their large, double, fragrant flowers grow one to a long stem. These roses were originally produced from crossings with the tea roses of China. They reached their high point at the beginning of this century. Their decline in favor was arrested by the arrival in 1945 of the hybrid tea "Gloria Dei," which provided new momentum for the next three decades. This healthy rose with especially large, double, yellow flowers astonished the rose world of the day.

Cluster-flowered Roses
The cluster-flowered roses—polyanthas and floribundas—have followed a triumphant course almost parallel with the hybrid teas.
Polyanthas. The polyantha roses had already been developed in France around 1875. They are small-flowered with large clusters of flowers and bloom all summer long.
Floribundas. Then, through crossing with the large-flowered roses, the polyantha hybrids appeared and since 1930 have been known as floribundas. The color palette quickly broadened from red and pink to dark red, white, salmon, crimson, lilac, and, with "Poulsen's Yellow" (1938), also to yellow.

There were double, semidouble, and single flowers of various sizes.
Spray roses. These grow vigorously upright and are particularly suitable for open areas. They are small, semidouble, and delicately colored. In addition, they are considered to keep for a long time and are not damaged by rain; however their leaves are not very healthy.
Grandifloras arose from the repeated crossing of hybrid teas with cluster-flowering varieties.

Miniature Roses
As with the small-flowered roses, there is every kind of variation today. The miniature roses have been crossed so frequently with polyanthas, musk hybrids, and floribundas that a distinction between them and the cluster-flowered roses is scarcely possible any longer.

A pathway bordered with fragrant bedding roses. The polyantha "Nathalie Nypels" with white centranthus, lavender blue catnip, and yellow green lady's-mantle in front of a yew hedge.

BEDDING ROSES

Mildred Scheel
Hybrid tea. Tantau 1976,
ADR Rose 1978.
Buds large, blackish red, cone-shaped, opening slender. Flowers deep velvety dark red; 3½ in. (9 cm) Ø, doubled, up to 40 petals; often borne on sturdy stems; unusually strong fragrance. Burns only in very strong sun. Sometimes rain hinders opening of buds, which then rot. Growth sturdy, up to 31 in. (80 cm) high, good new cane production. Foliage medium-sized and dense, intensely reddish when new, later dark green, dull, coarse. Use at distance of 14 in. (35 cm), seven plants per 11 sq ft (1 sq m).
  My tip: Long-lasting scented cut rose. Beautiful foliage.

Erotica
(= "Eroica")
Hybrid tea. Tantau 1969.
Buds oval, pointed. Flowers velvety dark red; very large at 5 in. (12 cm) Ø, well doubled with 33 petals, beautifully shaped, usually growing one to a long stem; pleasant, strong fragrance; luxuriant bloomer; quite rainfast and sunfast. Growth strong and upright, 31 in. (80 cm) high. Foliage dark green, red at first. Use at distance of 12 in. (30 cm), nine plants per 11 sq ft (1 sq m).
  My tip: Also suitable for cutting and as a standard.

Caribia
Hybrid tea. H. Wheatcroft 1973.
Buds long, pointed; tinted golden yellow to reddish. Flowers golden yellow with red-striped blazes; large at 3½ in. (9 cm) Ø; loosely doubled, 25 petals; situated alone on stiff stems; slightly fragrant; early blooming, good fall bloom. Growth sturdy and bushy, 27 in. (70 cm) high. Foliage medium-sized,

Mildred Scheel

Erotica

Caribia

medium green, slightly glossy. Use for bedding and groups; because of the highly original color combination a matter of taste. Spot anthracnose possible. Distance 14 in. (35 cm) apart or eight plants per 11 sq ft (1 sq m).

Hidalgo
Hybrid tea. Meilland 1979.
Buds long, cone-shaped, usually growing singly. Flowers velvety dark red, large-flowered, 5 in. (12 cm) Ø, well doubled, 40 petals; strongly scented; good repeat flowering. Growth strong, upright up to 39 in. (100 cm) high. Foliage very large, green, somewhat glossy. Use

Large-flowered (Hybrid Teas)

Hidalgo

Baronne Edmond de Rothschild

Burgund '81

Duftwolke

Burgund '81
Hybrid tea. Kordes 1981.
<u>Buds</u> large and pointed oval, opening spirally. <u>Flowers</u> glowing red, velvety; large, 5 in. (12 cm), very strongly doubled with 50 firm petals, elegant form; flowers single or several occurring together; rainfast within limits; slightly fragrant. <u>Growth</u> compact, upright and bushy, 27 in. (70 cm) high. <u>Foliage</u> medium-sized, matte green, reddish when new. <u>Use</u> 12 in. (30 cm) apart, nine plants per 11 sq ft (1 sq m).
My tip: Also very good for standards.

Duftwolke
(= "Fragrant Cloud")
Hybrid tea. Tantau 1963, ADR Rose 1964, World Rose 1981.
<u>Buds</u> pointed oval, bright red. <u>Flowers</u> intense orange red at first, later geranium red to purple red; large-flowered, up to 5 in. (12 cm) Ø; well doubled with 30 firm petals; often growing several to one long stem; intense fragrance. <u>Growth</u> sturdy, compact, upright, 31 in. (80 cm) high. <u>Foliage</u> dark green, large, leathery leaves. <u>Use</u> 14 in. (35 cm) apart, seven plants per 11 sq ft (1 sq m).
My tip: Occasionally attacked by spot anthracnose. Long-lasting flowers; also good for difficult locations. A fragrant rose of the first class. Unsprayed, the petals are good for rose punch. The flowers look somewhat plump.

12 in. (30 cm) apart, nine plants per 11 sq ft (1 sq m).
My tip: "Hidalgo" is also attractive as a cut rose because of its scent.

Baronne Edmond de Rothschild
Hybrid tea. Meilland 1969, ADR Rose 1971.
<u>Buds</u> pointed spherical, crimson red. <u>Flowers</u> deep ruby to crimson inside, shimmering silvery on the outside; very large at 5 in. (12 cm) Ø, luxuriant bloomer, intense fragrance. <u>Growth</u> very sturdy, 33 in. (85 cm) tall, good new cane production. <u>Foliage</u> very large, quite rainfast, leathery-coarse, bronze green, very glossy. <u>Use</u> 14 in. (35 cm) apart, seven plants per 11 sq ft (1 sq m).
My tip: An attractive, fragrant hybrid tea rose that also thrives well in difficult locations.

BEDDING ROSES

Sutter's Gold
Hybrid tea. Swim/Armstrong 1950. Buds long, elegant, with red markings. Flowers light orange yellow, especially outside more or less strongly reddish, veined or washed with coppery color, later fading a good deal. Medium-sized, 3 in. (8 cm), loosely but well doubled with 35 petals; blooming heavily, usually one to a stem, strongly scented. Growth sturdy, stiffly upright, branching, 35 in. (90 cm) high. Foliage medium-sized, glossy. Use 12 in. (30 cm) apart, nine plants per 11 sq ft (1 sq m).
   My tip: Also popular as a rose for cutting.

Sutter's Gold

Alexander
("Alexandra" in Switzerland)
Hybrid tea. Harkness 1972, ADR Rose 1974.
Buds oval, tile red. Flowers light orange to vermilion red; large, 3½ in. (9 cm) Ø; loosely doubled with 23 petals, one or several to a long stem; slightly fragrant, self-cleaning. Growth very strong, upright and 35 in. (90 cm) high. Very striking bent thorns, light, large, broad at the base, running to a point; densely situated. Foliage almost dark green with a little red, glossy. Use 14 in. (35 cm) apart, seven plants per 11 sq ft (1 sq m).
   My tip: Suitable as a cut rose. Not entirely healthy anymore.

Alexander

Elina
Hybrid tea. P. Dickson/Pekmez 1983, ADR Rose 1987.
Buds elongated, greenish yellow. Flowers light primrose yellow; very large, 5½ in. (14 cm) Ø, 34 petals, sturdy stems, long-lasting, blooms constantly and luxuriantly, weak scent. Growth sturdy and bushy, 31 in. (80 cm) high. Foliage quite

Elina

thick, large, glossy, dark green, oval leaflets, medium-sized thorns. Use 14 in. (35 cm) apart, seven plants per 11 sq ft (1 sq m).
   My tip: Very resistant to spot anthracnose, mildew, and rust. Excellent rose for cutting.

Whisky

Whisky
Hybrid tea. Tantau 1967.
Buds pointed oval to slender, yellow. Flowers amber yellow; large, 4 in. (11 cm) Ø, well doubled, 25 slightly wavy petals, elegant; strong, pleasing scent. Keeps blooming until fall. Growth sturdy, bushy, branching, fast production of new canes, 35 in. (90 cm) high. Foliage large, red when first appearing, later dark green, dense.
   My tip: Only sometimes somewhat prone to mildew. The red new growth with the amber-colored, fragrant flowers is magnificent until frost. Summer pruning is recommended.

Large-flowered (Hybrid Teas)

Banzai '83

Chopin

Gloria Dei

Chopin

Hybrid tea. Stanislaw Zyla 1990/91.
Buds large, round, golden yellow.
Flowers yellow with apricot; medium-sized, 3½ in. (9 cm) Ø; loosely doubled, 25 petals; one or several growing on one stem; good scent; good production of new growth. Growth very strong, 47 in. (120 cm) high, stiffly upright, bush falls apart slightly. Foliage large, dark green, glossy. Use in groups. Distance 16 in. (40 cm) apart, six plants per 11 sq ft (1 sq m).
 My tip: Very vital variety.

Gloria Dei

(= "Mme A. Meilland," Peace," "Gioia")
Hybrid tea. Meilland 1945, World Rose 1976.
Buds plump, broadly cone-shaped, yellow with red veins; beautiful sepals. Flowers golden yellow, later lighter yellow and intense pink; very large flowers, 6 in. (15 cm) Ø, with some 50 petals, densely but loosely doubled, cup-shaped, on very sturdy stems, lightly scented. Continuous flowering, richly decorative flowers. Growth sturdy, becoming over 39 in. (100 cm) high, very sturdy canes. Foliage very large, deep green, extremely glossy, coarse, robust. Use in many different ways, also alone. Distance 16 to 18 in. (40–45 cm) apart, five to six plants per 11 sq ft (1 sq m).
 My tip: Good for cutting; keeps a long time once cut.

Banzai '83

Hybrid tea. Meilland 1983, ADR Rose 1985.
Buds pointed oval, yellow with red markings. Flowers golden yellow, orange along the edges; 4 in. (10 cm) Ø, very double, 35 petals, round; usually rainfast, delicate fragrance. Growth sturdy, stiff, twiggy, yet bushy, in fall keeps growing without flowering. Height 35 in. (90 cm). Foliage dark green, leathery, glossy. Use 14 in. (35 cm) apart, seven plants per 11 sq ft (1 sq m).
 My tip: Quite resistant but in late summer an attack of spot anthracnose can appear quite easily. Fertilize in May.

BEDDING ROSES

Piroschka

Hybrid tea. Tantau 1972.
<u>Buds</u> oval, pointed. <u>Flowers</u> pure pink, large, 3 in. (8 cm) Ø, loosely doubled with 30 petals, cup-shaped going to flat; several together on one stem; strong, magnificent fragrance. <u>Growth</u> bushy, 23 in. (60 cm) high. <u>Foliage</u> red brown at first, then medium green, decorative. <u>Use</u> 16 in. (40 cm) apart, five to seven plants per 11 sq ft (1 sq m). Very well-suited for standards.

Alte Liebe

Hybrid tea. GPG Roter Oktober 1974.
<u>Buds</u> oval to urn-shaped. <u>Flowers</u> salmon red, lighter at the center but darkening as flowers fade; large at 5 in. (12 cm) Ø, loosely doubled with 25 petals, chalice-shaped, often several on one stem, late-blooming. <u>Growth</u> broad-upright, 35 in. (90 cm) high. <u>Foliage</u> dark green with gloss. <u>Use</u> 16 in. (40 cm) apart, six plants per 11 sq ft (1 sq m).
   My tip: Note the rose's later flowering time. Also very attractive and long-lasting in the vase. More good varieties: "<u>Basilika</u>" (pink), "<u>Citrina</u>" (golden yellow), and "<u>Bonjour</u>" (crimson).

Pascali

Hybrid tea. Lens 1963, World Rose 1991.
<u>Buds</u> slender, classic, delicate greenish white; with elegant sepals. <u>Flowers</u> pure white; large, 3 in. (8 cm) Ø; well doubled with 30 petals, classic form, ultimately flat, occurring singly or in small, loose bunches; without scent; very heavy bloomer. <u>Growth</u> sturdy, well branched, bushy, strong cane production, 27 in. (30 cm) high. <u>Foliage</u> light green at first, then deep

Piroschka

green, with gloss. <u>Use</u> 14 in. (35 cm) apart, seven plants per 11 sq ft (1 sq m).
   My tip: Good in the garden with perennials, also good as a cut flower.

Alte Liebe

Pascali

Aachener Dom

Hawaiian Sunset

Evening Star

Blue River

Hawaiian Sunset

Hybrid tea. Swim & Weeks 1962.
Buds round-oval, light red. Flowers coppery orange with yellow edge; large, 4 in. (10 cm) Ø, well doubled with 30 petals, develops flat, usually one to a stiff stem, good fragrance. Growth bushy, compact, 23 in. (60 cm) high. Foliage very large, robust, dark green, dense and abundant. Use singly or in beds, also for cutting. Distance 16 in. (40 cm) apart, six plants per 11 sq ft (1 sq m). Also recommended: "Circus Knie," 31 in. (80 cm) high, quite healthy.

My tip: Not very disease- or pest-prone. Warm, glowing color but difficult to place near perennials. Good for standard.

Aachener Dom

Hybrid tea. Meilland 1982, ADR Rose 1982.
Buds round, fat. Flowers silvery salmon pink; quite large, 4 in. (10 cm) Ø, densely doubled with 40 petals, usually in tight bunches or deep in the foliage; pleasing scent. Good repeat flowering; rain can hinder development of buds and produce balling. Growth strongly upright, but sufficiently branching, bush of 27 in. (70 cm) in height. Foliage very coarse, large-leaved, dark green, leathery. Use 12 in. (30 cm) apart, nine plants per 11 sq ft (1 sq m).

Evening Star

Hybrid tea. Jackson & Perkins/ Kordes 1974.
Buds yellow, long, pointed, opening spirally. Flowers cream white to white; large, 4 in. (10 cm) Ø, well doubled with 25 petals, cup-shaped, occurring in groups of several or one to a stem, well-scented, self-cleaning. Not entirely rainfast, forms balls. Growth very sturdy, upright-bushy, 35 in. (90 cm) high, good cane production. Foliage deep green, large, leathery. Use 12 in. (30 cm) apart, 9 plants per 11 sq ft (1 sq m).

My tip: In late summer, often considerable spot anthracnose infection. Sensitive to prolonged rain.

Blue River

Hybrid tea. Kordes 1984.
Buds medium-sized, round-oval. Flowers magenta lavender, darker around the edges; medium-sized, 3 in. (8 cm) Ø, classically shaped, well doubled with 30 petals, usually growing several to a bunch; very strong, delicious fragrance. Growth bushy, branching, medium-high, 27 in. (70 cm). Foliage medium-sized, dark green with gloss. Use for bedding and in mixed plantings. Distance 14 in. (35 cm) apart, eight plants per 11 sq ft (1 sq m).

My tip: Robust but, like all varieties in this color group, somewhat prone to spot anthracnose. Very attractive as a cut flower. The variety was awarded the Gold Medal in Baden-Baden for its perfume.

BEDDING ROSES

Maria Mathilda
Floribunda. Lens 1980.
Buds slender, elegant. Flowers white, lightly shaded with pale pink; medium-sized at 3 in. (7 cm) Ø, hybrid tea shape, semidouble, 20 petals; little fragrance; good continuous, heavy flowering. Growth sturdy, 27 in. (70 cm) high. Foliage dark green with gloss. Use 14 in. (35 cm) apart, seven plants per 11 sq ft (1 sq m). Also recommended: "Edelweiss," semidouble rosette, very heavy bloomer; only 20 in. (50 cm) high; and "Kristall" (GPG Roter Oktober 1979), white with cream-colored center, 25 in. (65 cm) high.

My tip: Somewhat prone to spot anthracnose in fall. Very harmonious flowers; also an attractive cut rose.

La Sevillana
Floribunda. Meilland 1978, ADR Rose 1979.
Buds bloodred, broad, cone-shaped. Flowers brilliant red; medium-sized, 3 in. (7 cm) Ø, semidouble, with some 15 petals, growing in groups of 3–5 on long, limber stems; scentless; ever-blooming; somewhat sensitive to rain. Growth high, branching like a wild rose, loosely bushy, 31 in. (80 cm) high. Foliage medium-sized, dark green, glossy. Use for hedges, individual plantings with shrubs; distance 14 in. (35 cm) apart, seven plants per 11 sq ft (1 sq m).

My tip: "La Sevillana" is much healthier than the rose-toned "Pink La Sevillana."

Maria Mathilda

La Sevillana

Kleine Dortmund

Kleine Dortmund
Floribunda. Noack 1992.
Buds small, pointed oval, red. Flowers light red with white centers and yellow stamens; quite small, $^3/_4$–1 in. (2–3 cm) Ø, single, up to 50 in one cluster; little scent; late flowering but blooms until October. Growth bushy, 23 in. (60 cm) high, continued growth from inside out. Foliage light green, medium-sized, leathery, glossy. Use for beds and areas. Distance 16 in. (40 cm) apart, six plants per 11 sq ft (1 sq m).

My tip: When using "Kleine Dortmund" as a ground cover, there should be at least five plants per 11 sq ft (1 sq m). Very healthy.

Montana

Margaret Merril

Montana
Floribunda. Tantau 1974, ADR Rose 1974.
Buds dark red, stumpy cone-shaped to cup-shaped, several in thick clusters. Flowers glowing red, colorfast, medium-sized, 3 in. (7 cm) Ø, saucer-shaped, semidouble with 25 somewhat wavy petals; no scent; weatherfast. Growth strong, erectly upright. Foliage good medium size, dense, reddish when sprouting, later very glossy dark green, leathery. Use as robust bedding and border rose. Distance 16 in. (40 cm) apart, six plants per 11 sq ft (1 sq m). Also recommended: "Tornado" (ADR Rose 1972), "Olala" (ADR Rose 1956), still healthy, and "Neues Europa" (ADR Rose 1964) in different shades of red.

My tip: Usually some spot anthracnose appears. Fertilize again in May.

Cluster-flowered (Floribundas)

cm) high. Foliage reddish when sprouting, soon glossy green, medium-sized. Use as bedding and group rose of very distinctive, fine color. Also good with perennials. Distance 14 in. (35 cm) apart, seven plants per 11 sq ft (1 sq m).

My tip: Usually some spot anthracnose appears. First class as a standard and very healthy.

Schneeflocke
Floribunda. Noack 1991,
ADR Rose 1991.
Buds white, fat, and longish when opening. Flowers pure white, small, 2 in. (5 cm) Ø, full semidoubled with 16 petals, up to 20 in a cluster growing on one stem; some fragrance; very heavy bloomer, weatherfast. Growth broadly bushy, 20 in. (50 cm) high, good continuing growth. Foliage deep-green, medium-sized, glossy. Use in groups and for areas. Distance 23 in. (60 cm) apart, 3 plants per 11 sq ft (1 sq m).

My tip: Very disease-resistant; continuous bloomer on good soil.

Papagena
Floribunda. McGredy/Rosenunion 1989.
Buds oval. Flowers red with irregular broad white stripes "hand-painted" like the parrot tulip species; large, 3 in. (8 cm) Ø, loosely double with 15 petals, occurring in clusters. Growth bushy, compact, 23 in. (60 cm) high. Foliage dark green, glossy. Use for borders with a distinctive character. Distance 14 in. (35 cm) apart, eight plants per 11 sq ft (1 sq m).

My tip: Not disease-hardy. Striped roses are a delicate, very individual matter of taste.

Schneeflocke

Papagena

Margaret Merril
Floribunda. Harkness 1980.
Buds pale pink, long, pointed, opening spirally. Flowers pearl white with pink overcast; large, 3½ in. (9 cm) Ø, semidouble with especially beautiful open center, 20 slightly wavy petals; outstanding, intense fragrance. Good repeat flowering. Growth moderate, upright, broadly shrubby up to 23 in. (60

BEDDING ROSES

Friesia
Floribunda. Kordes 1973, ADR Rose 1973.
Buds intense yellow, oval, pointed. Flowers glowing yellow, color very weatherfast, not even fading as flowers wither; unfolds like a hybrid tea but only medium-sized at $2^3/_4$ in. (7 cm) Ø; loosely doubled with 20–25 petals. Occurs in clusters of several; good, pleasing scent. Good repeat flowering; self-cleaning. Growth medium vigor, upright, but well branched, 16 in. (40 cm) high. Foliage medium-sized, glossy green. Use 16 in. (40 cm) apart, six plants per 11 sq ft (1 sq m).
My tip: Rewarding everbloomer with scent and good color maintenance. Suitable for good soils. "Friesia" is an attractive cut flower, also good as a standard.

Pigalle '85
Floribunda. Meilland 1985.
Buds roundish, large. Flowers coppery yellow inside, flamed orange outside; large flowers, 4 in. (10 cm) Ø, densely doubled with 50 petals; blooming in bunches and very luxuriantly. Growth vigorously bushy, 16–23 in. (40–60 cm) high. Foliage medium to deep green. Use in a small group, harmonizes well with blue perennials. Distance 14 in. (35 cm) apart, eight plants per 11 sq ft (1 sq m).
My tip: Orange red roses are loved by a great many people, certainly, but they go badly with other rose colors.

Friesia

Pigalle '85

Goldener Sommer

Apricot Nectar

Goldener Sommer '83
Floribunda. Noack 1983, ADR Rose 1985.
Buds large, broadly cone-shaped, golden yellow. Flowers gold to mimosa yellow, lighter toward the edges; large-flowered, 3 in. (8 cm) Ø, double with 20 petals; flowers occur alone or in small clusters,

heavy bloomer; little fragrance. Not always entirely self-cleaning, since after much rain the flowers ball. Growth moderately vigorous, branching from the bottom to form a wide bush. Foliage medium-sized, light green and, later, medium green, matte, somewhat leathery. Use 16 in. (40 cm) apart, six plants per 11 sq ft (1 sq m).
My tip: Shows to best effect against a dark background of trees.

Cluster-flowered (Floribundas)

Amber Queen

Goldquelle

Badener Gold

Apricot Nectar

Floribunda. Boerner/Jackson & Perkins 1965.
<u>Buds</u> elongated, oval. <u>Flowers</u> apricot; large, 4 in. (10 cm) Ø, well doubled; several flowers to one stem; delicate tea rose fragrance. Good fall bloomer, very long-lasting. <u>Growth</u> compact but sturdy, bushy, 31 in. (80 cm) high. <u>Foliage</u> deep green, glossy. <u>Use</u> as bedding and group rose for individual gardens. Distance 16 in. (40 cm) apart, six plants every 11 sq ft (1 sq m).

   My tip: Very healthy and robust. Also very attractive as a cut flower. Charming color.

Amber Queen

Shrub rose/Floribunda.
Harkness 1984, Golden Rose of Den Haag 1991.
<u>Buds</u> cone-shaped to oval, brownish yellow. <u>Flowers</u> deep amber yellow at first, light amber in full bloom; medium-sized at $2^3/_4$ in. (7 cm) Ø, double, with 30 petals, occurring in small bunches; lightly scented. <u>Growth</u> broadly shrubby, 16–23 in. (40–60 cm) high. <u>Foliage</u> light green, glossy. <u>Use</u> at intervals of 18 in. (45 cm) apart, 5 plants per 11 sq ft (1 sq m).

   My tip: A charmingly colored, beautifully shaped, and healthy rose.

Goldquelle

Floribunda. Tantau 1988.
<u>Buds</u> like a hybrid tea. <u>Flowers</u> golden yellow, medium-sized, 3 in. (8 cm) Ø, loosely doubled, stamens show when opened; situated in large bunches; little scent. Flowering season extends to late August. Keeps well. <u>Growth</u> sturdy, upright, bushy, 27 in. (70 cm) high. <u>Foliage</u> glossy, fresh green. <u>Use</u> as bedding and group rose, alone. Distance 14 in. (35 cm) apart, eight plants per 11 sq ft (1 sq m).

Badener Gold

Floribunda. McGredy/Rosenunion 1974.
<u>Buds</u> elegant, pointed oval. <u>Flowers</u> golden orange with light red shading; 4 in. (9 cm) Ø, loosely doubled; some scent. Early and luxuriant bloomer, self-cleaning. <u>Growth</u> well branched, 27 in. (70 cm) high, continues to produce new canes. <u>Foliage</u> deep green, glossy. <u>Use</u> as bedding and group rose, for borders. Distance 14 in. (35 cm) apart, eight plants per 11 sq ft (1 sq m).

   My tip: Somewhat prone to spot anthracnose.

BEDDING ROSES

Queen Elizabeth

Floribunda. Lammerts 1954, World Rose 1979.

<u>Buds</u> light red, hybrid-tea-rose-like, large, elongated, single or in groups of 3–7. <u>Flowers</u> salmon pink at first, opening pure pink, finally paling. Large-flowered, 3 to 4 in. (8–10 cm) Ø, cup-shaped, loosely doubled, 20–25 petals; in bunches of 3–9 on long stems. Everblooming; but barely fragrant. <u>Growth</u> very sturdy, erectly upright, 39–70 in. (100 to 180 cm) high. Few, large thorns. <u>Foliage</u> very large, loose, reddish to dark green, coarse, glossy. <u>Use</u> in isolated groups with perennials, for borders, hedges. Distance 18 in. (45 cm) apart, five plants per 11 sq ft (1 sq m).

My tip: Healthy, robust, some mildew in fall. Avoid the bare branches below by pruning in stages or using it as a "background rose," putting perennials or small shrub roses in front of it. Also very attractive in a vase.

Queen Elizabeth

Sommerwind

Märchenland

Sommerwind

Floribunda. Kordes 1985, ADR Rose 1987.

<u>Buds</u> oval, pointed, dark rose to red. <u>Flowers</u> brilliant rose; medium-sized, 2 in. (6 cm) Ø, loosely doubled, 12 wavy, scalloped petals, several flowers in a cluster; little fragrance; blooms abundantly until frost. <u>Growth</u> broadly shrubby, very branching, 20–23 in. (50–60 cm) high. <u>Foliage</u> luxuriant, medium green, small, glossy. <u>Use</u> 14 in. (35 cm) apart, seven plants per 11 sq ft (1 sq m).

My tip: Usually some mildew, very robust. Charming as a standard rose ("mophead").

Betty Prior

Märchenland

Floribunda. Tantau 1946.

<u>Buds</u> pale cherry red, broadly cone-shaped, several in loose bunches. <u>Flowers</u> pink with salmon tinge, fading to light pink; medium-sized, 3–3$\frac{1}{2}$ in. (8–9 cm) Ø, semidouble, 20 petals, saucer-shaped; weak scent. Good repeat flowering. <u>Growth</u> arching broadly shrubby,

well branched. Inflorescence sometimes upright, sometimes drooping. Height 31–47 in. (80–120 cm). <u>Foliage</u> medium-sized, glossy green, reddish at first. <u>Use</u> as bedding, group, or small shrub rose, with perennials or in front of shrubs. Distance 18 in. (45 cm) apart, five plants per 11 sq ft (1 sq m).

My tip: Highly recommended. Some mildew in the fall.

Betty Prior

Floribunda. Prior 1935.

<u>Buds</u> oval, crimson red, elegant sepals. <u>Flowers</u> crimson on the outside, lighter inside, with white-pink centers; medium-sized, around 2 in. (4–6 cm) Ø, single, 5 broad petals, saucer-shaped, in

Cluster-flowered (Floribundas)

Bonica '82

Bonica '82

Floribunda. Meilland 1982, ADR Rose 1982.

Buds roundish, dark pink. Flowers pink at first with a soft salmon tone, later opening pure pink, lighter pink as it fades. Medium-sized, 3 in. (7 cm), doubled with 25 petals; in bunches of 10–20. Good repeat bloomer, lasts a long time. Growth broadly shrubby, well branched, dense in late summer, often over 27 in. (70 cm) high. Foliage small, dark green, leathery-glossy. Use also as a ground cover and conceivably as a small shrub rose. Distance 18 in. (45 cm) apart, five plants per 11 sq ft.

Play Rose

Floribunda. Meilland 1989, ADR Rose 1989.

Buds broadly conical, dark pink. Flowers strong crimson pink to pure pink; large, 3–3$\frac{1}{2}$ in. (8–9 cm) Ø, 15 petals, loosely doubled, often quartered in the center; groups of several, heavy-blooming. Growth moderately strong, bushy, upright, 27 in. (70 cm) high, in fall over 39 in. (100 cm) with budless canes. Foliage medium green, semiglossy, medium-sized. Use also as a ground cover. Distance 23 in. (60 cm) apart, three plants per 11 sq ft (1 sq m).

My tip: Robust, unpretentious; a bit prone to spot anthracnose, some mildew in late summer.

Ricarda

Floribunda. Noack 1989, ADR Rose 1989.

Buds fat and compact, light red. Flowers vermilion red; small, 2$\frac{3}{4}$ in. (7 cm) Ø, slightly doubled, 16 petals, wavy edges, rainfast, self-cleaning. Growth stiffly erect, 31 in. (80 cm) high. Foliage small. Use 14 in. (35 cm) apart, seven plants per 11 sq ft (1 sq m).

Play Rose

Ricarda

quite large umbrella-shaped bunches; no scent. Luxuriant and everblooming. Rainfast and self-cleaning. Growth slender, upright, broad at the top, 31 in. (80 cm) high. Foliage large, very red when first appearing, later green, dull, covers well. Use 16–18 in. (40–45 cm) apart, five to six plants per 11 sq ft (1 sq m).

My tip: Healthy; in dry years some mildew possible in late summer. Suitable next to shrub borders and with perennials, since it will tolerate semishade. Beautiful rose for mixed borders.

BEDDING ROSES

Diadem

Floribunda (so-called "Spray rose"). Tantau 1986.

<u>Buds</u> round and compact, dark pink. <u>Flowers</u> slightly bluish light pink; medium-sized, 3 in. (8 cm) Ø; semidouble, 18 petals, classically shaped; several on long, straight stems; no scent. <u>Growth</u> sturdily upright and branching, 35 in. (90 cm) high. <u>Foliage</u> reddish at first, then dark green, medium-sized. <u>Use</u> 14 in. (35 cm) apart, seven plants per 11 sq ft (1 sq m).

My tip: Winter-hardy, some spot anthracnose possible in late summer. In summer, prune often; a distinctive cut flower.

Zwergkönig '78

Miniature rose. Kordes 1978.

<u>Buds</u> small, fat, and pointed oval; velvety bloodred, open like hybrid tea. <u>Flowers</u> brilliant bloodred with velvety gloss, unfolding with open yellow center; color holds well, even in sun, but in heat it becomes blackish red from the edge inward. Large, 2 in. (5–6 cm) Ø, loosely doubled; a few at the ends of numerous short canes; almost no fragrance. Repeats well. <u>Growth</u> upright, moderately vigorous, up to 20 in. (50 cm) high, but well branched; continues to produce new growth well. <u>Foliage</u> dark green. <u>Use</u> 12 in. (30 cm) apart, nine plants per 11 sq ft (1 sq m).

Guletta

(= "Rugull," "Tapis Jaune") Miniature rose.
de Ruiter 1976/Rosenunion.

<u>Buds</u> relatively large, fat, with points, lemon yellow. <u>Flowers</u> lemon yellow; after opening, the center becomes distinctly lighter; large, 2 in. (5 cm) Ø, semidouble, 20 petals, classic; dense, branching

Diadem

inflorescences of varying heights; without fragrance. Blooms abundantly and often and flowers keep. <u>Growth</u> moderately strong, fatly shrubby, not compact, up to 14 in. (35 cm) high. <u>Foliage</u> small, light green to medium green leaves, charming small leaflets, slightly glossy. Prone to leaf-drop. <u>Use</u> 10 in. (25 cm) apart, 12 plants per 11 sq ft (1 sq m).

Zwergkönig '78

Guletta

Vatertag

My tip: Most attractive because of its very heavy reblooming, long duration, and glowing color.

Vatertag

Polyantha. Tantau 1959. Sport of "Muttertag" and thereby apparently the last representative of a remarkable chain of seven sports that is supposed to go back to the climbing rose "Tausendschön" by Kiese/J. C. Schmidt 1906.
Buds small, roundish, orange. Flowers orange, small, 1 in. (3 cm) Ø, spherical, loosely doubled with 25 petals; in June up to 30 in a cluster, fewer in later flowering; almost no fragrance. Growth bushy, branching, low, 14 in. (35 cm) high, good new cane production. Foliage light green, somewhat glossy, leaflets small, narrow, pointed. Use as dwarf and pot rose, for borders, groups, cemetery plantings, also for planters on balconies. Distance 12 in. apart, 11 plants per 11 sq ft (1 sq m). Also recommended: Other members of the "sport family" are "Muttertag,"

Climbing Pompon de Paris

Baby Masquerade

Zwergkönigin '82

brilliant red; "Dick Koster," pale pink; "Margo Koster," salmon pink; "Sneprinsesse," white.

Pompon de Paris

Miniature rose. Before 1823. "Rouletii" around 1920. Both most probably identical.
Buds round. Flowers rose red with some lilac; small, about an inch (2–3 cm) Ø, very double rosette, 30 petals, spherical, one alone or several together; some fragrance. Heavy bloomer, repeats well until November. Not rainfast: flowers ball. Hips less than $\frac{1}{2}$ in. (1 cm) Ø, round, orange, lasting. Growth bushy, branching. Plant grown from cutting is 6 in. (15 cm) high, a

grafted one twice as large. Foliage slender oval with extended point, dull dark green. Use as a planter rose; also as a dwarf rose in groups in the garden. Also recommended: **"Climbing Pompon de Paris"** grows to a height of 23 in. (60 cm) and is very good as a small shrub rose for the garden—in groups or alone. Decorative hips can be sacrificed to promote sturdier canes: summer pruning!
My tip: Growth continues well despite spot anthracnose.

Baby Masquerade

Miniature rose. Tantau 1955.
Buds small, oval, red. Flowers golden yellow at first, then gradually glowing red, two-toned; small, 1 in. (3 cm) Ø, shallow, with 20 wavy petals; scarcely any scent. Good repeat blooming. Growth bushy, branching, sturdy, up to 20 in. (50 cm) high. Foliage small, deep green, matte, dense. Use for high beds, tubs, and balconies.
My tip: Good to propagate through cuttings. Unfortunately, prone to disease. Always cut off faded clusters to hasten reflowering.

Zwergkönigin '82

Miniature rose. Kordes 1982.
Buds small, roundish, red. Flowers deep rose; very large, 3 in. (7 cm) Ø, looks like the hybrid tea rose, loosely doubled, 24 petals, always in clusters of several; scarcely any scent. Keeps very well. Growth sturdy, bushy, well branched, height up to 20 in. (50 cm). Foliage small, dark green and very glossy. Use 12 in. (30 cm) apart, nine plants per 11 sq ft (1 sq m).
My tip: Healthier than "Zwergkönig."

BEDDING ROSES

Variety	Grower/Year	Flower	Height in in. (cm)	Remarks
Large-flowered Roses—Hybrid Teas				
Alec's Red	Cocker 1970	cherry red, 4¼ in. (11 cm) Ø, double	35 (90)	Strong fragrance, cutting rose.
Basilika	VEB Saatzucht Dresden 1981	intense pink, 5 in. (13 cm) Ø, double	35 (90)	Fragrant, heavy flowering until October.
Berolina	Kordes 1986	yellow, somewhat reddish, 4 in. (10 cm) Ø, double	31 (80)	Strongly scented, also good for cutting. ADR Rose 1986.
Citrina	VEB Saatzucht Dresden 1981	golden yellow, 4¼ in. (11 cm) Ø, double	39 (100)	Self-cleaning, some fragrance.
Double Delight	Swim 1978	cream white, red, 5 in. (13 cm) Ø, double	16 (40)	Spicy scent, World Rose 1986.
Duftstern	Noack 1973	salmon pink orange, 4 in. (10 cm) Ø, double	27 (70)	Strong fragrance, good as standard.
Florentina	Kordes 1973	dark red, 4¾ in. (12 cm) Ø, semidouble	47 (120)	Upright growth, fragrant.
Helmut Schmidt	Kordes 1979	light yellow, 3½ in. (9 cm) Ø, semidouble	27 (70)	Stiff growth, slight scent, cutting rose.
Henkell Royal	Kordes 1964	bloodred, 4¼ in. (11 cm) Ø, semidouble	31 (80)	Upright growth, very strong fragrance.
Ingrid Bergmann	Olesen/ Poulsen 1983	dark red, 4¾ in. (12 cm) Ø, loosely doubled	27 (70)	Pleasing fragrance, luxuriant bloomer.
Julius Rose	Wisbech Plant Co. 1976	lilac brownish, 3 in. (8 cm) Ø, loosely doubled	31 (80)	Unusual color, delicate.
Lady Rose	Kordes 1979	salmon orange, 5 in. (13 cm) Ø, double	27 (70)	Bushy growth, large foliage, glossy, faint fragrance.
Landora	Tantau 1970	golden yellow, 4 in. (10 cm) Ø, loosely doubled	27 (70)	Sturdy growth, somewhat delicate.
Lolita	Kordes 1972	orange yellow, 4 in. (10 cm) Ø, semidouble	27 (70)	Upright growth, strong fragrance, ADR Rose 1973.
Luci Cramphorn	Kriloff 1960	geranium red, 4¾ in. (12 cm) Ø, double	31 (80)	Stiff growth, good fragrance.
Michèle Meilland	Meilland 1945	rose salmon, 4 in. (10 cm) Ø, semidouble	35 (90)	Upright growth, good scent, beautiful, very tender.
Norita	Combe/ Vilmorin 1966	black red, 4 in. (10 cm) Ø, semidouble	20 (50)	Upright growth, good scent, everblooming.
Oklahoma	Swim & Weeks 1964	black red, 4¾ in. (12 cm) Ø, double	31 (80)	Bushy growth, strong fragrance, classic buds.
Olympiad	MacGredy/ Armstrong 1985	red, 5½ in. (14 cm) Ø, double	23 (60)	Light scent, suitable for standard.

Variety	Grower/Year	Flower	Height in in. (cm)	Remarks
Peter Frankenfeld	Kordes 1966	rose red, 4 in. (10 cm) Ø, loosely doubled	35 (90)	Vigorous, long-stemmed, quite healthy.
Pink Favorite	Abrams 1956	pure pink, 3¹/₂ in. (9 cm) Ø, loosely doubled	31 (80)	Little scent, extremely healthy, balling possible.
Polarstern	Tantau 1982	white, 4¹/₄ in. (11 cm) Ø, double	39 (100)	Bushy growth, fragrant, heavy bloomer.
Rebecca	Tantau 1970	yellow/red, 4 in. (10 cm) Ø, semidouble	27 (70)	Bushy growth, ADR Rose 1972.
Rose Hans Rosenthal	Meilland 1987	dark red, 4¹/₄ in. (11 cm) Ø, densely doubled	27 (70)	Resistant to disease, undemanding.
The McCartney Rose	Meilland 1991	pink, 4¹/₄ in. (11 cm) Ø, loosely double	27 (70)	Good, strong scent.

Cluster-flowered Roses—Floribundas

Variety	Grower/Year	Flower	Height in in. (cm)	Remarks
Andalusien	Kordes 1977	bloodred, 3 in. (8 cm) Ø, loosely doubled	35 (90)	Bushy growth, gracefully drooping flowers, ADR Rose 1976.
Bella Rosa	Kordes 1982	salmon pink, 2¹/₄ in. (6 cm) Ø, loosely doubled	23 (60)	Bushy growth, begins flowering late, then everblooming.
Blue Parfum	Tantau 1978	lavender violet, 3¹/₂ in. (9 cm) Ø, semidouble	20 (50)	Bushy, compact growth, very strong scent, spot anthracnose.
Bernsteinrose	Tantau 1987	orange yellow, 3¹/₂ in. (9 cm) Ø, double	27 (70)	Romantic in fullness and color.
Chorus	Meilland 1975	vermilion red, 4 in. (10 cm) Ø, semidouble	27 (70)	ADR Rose 1977, since then not so robust.
Dalli-Dalli	Tantau 1977	dark red, 2³/₄ in. (7 cm) Ø, semidouble	27 (70)	ADR Rose 1975, heavy bloomer, upright-bushy growth.
Dolly	Poulsen 1975	dark pink, 2³/₄ in. (7 cm) Ø, semidouble	27 (70)	Bushy growth, open center, ADR Rose 1987.
Escapade	Harkness 1967	lavender pink, center lighter, 3 in. (8 cm) Ø, semidouble	31 (80)	Rare pastel color, ADR Rose 1973, light-green foliage.
Frau Astrid Späth	Späth 1930	crimson pink, 2¹/₄ in. (6 cm) Ø, semidouble	16 (40)	Sport of "Joseph Guy." Continuous-bloomer, somewhat disease-prone.
Happy Wanderer	MacGredy 1974	dark red, 2³/₄ in. (7 cm) Ø, double	16 (40)	Light scent, ADR Rose 1975, compact growth.
Joseph Guy	Nonin 1921	crimson pink, 3 in. (8 cm) Ø, semidouble	16 (40)	Bushy growth, giant inflorescences, long-lasting.
Make up	Meilland	salmon pink, 1¹/₂ in. (4 cm) Ø, double	31 (80)	Very long-lasting, also good for difficult conditions.

Standards (Tree Roses) and
CASCADES

These two specialties share a lack of natural origins, for they are both the result of the gardener's abilities. A "variety" is grafted onto a stem, or stock, of wild rose. Depending on the height of this stock, we differentiate between full, semi-, and quarter standards.

Cascade Roses

These are climbing roses grafted to stocks. Ramblers—that is, soft-caned varieties—are best suited for this purpose. The best are those that bloom repeatedly—and thus whose vigor of growth is inhibited—like "Super Excelsa," "Super Dorothy," or "Hermann Schmidt."

Stronger-growing varieties develop gorgeous cascade trees in the first five years, but so far there is no experience with them over longer periods. Thinning is important (see page 41).

Using stiff, vigorously growing climbers like "Sympathie" on standards is a mistake. On the other hand, stiff, moderately growing standards like "Rosarium Uetersen" develop a crown that spreads, to be sure, but that stays within bounds and is constantly in bloom. Once-blooming rambler varieties flower on wood from the previous year. They are already forming "green crowns" of this year's flowerless canes to be ready to bloom next year. These should never be mistaken for wild shoots and removed, for they will produce the most beautiful flowers next year.

Important: Cascade roses cannot be "laid down" for the winter like standards. They must be protected with fir boughs or burlap (see page 38).

Standards

Standards, or tree roses, are large-flowered or cluster-flowered roses that have been grafted onto a stock. Anyone choosing a hybrid tea, fragrant if possible, like "Manou Meilland," "Margaret Merril," "Blessings," or other compactly growing hybrid tea will be delighted.

Smaller repeat-flowering ground covers and floribundas are also very beautiful on standards. Thus "Snow Ballet" and "Swany" develop pretty round or half-round crowns, but so do "Sommerwind," "Schneewittchen," and "Yesterday." Because of the wide space between soil and crown, standard roses are scarcely affected by spot anthracnose at all, in contrast to bedding roses.

Standards with large-flowered or cluster-flowered varieties are pruned back hard in the spring. During the first ten years they can be "laid down" for the winter without requiring anything else (see KNOW-HOW, page 39).

In the picture below, cascade roses in a square. Here "Raubritter" with its globe-shaped flowers has been grafted onto short standards. In the picture to the right the rambler rose "Paul Noel"—grafted onto a full standard—likewise forms captivating cascades, and it is intensely fragrant.

STANDARDS

Kew Rambler

Climbing rose. Kew Gardens 1912.
Buds small, round, apricot. Flowers delicate salmon pink, lighter inside; small, 1 in. (2.5 cm) Ø, single, in large bunches; light fragrance. Blooms once, but very lushly. Growth sturdy, 195 in. (500 cm) high, overhanging. Foliage yellow green, later graying, medium-sized. Use as climbing rose on arbors. As cascade rose the "bell" achieves the extra-large size of 117 in. (300 cm) Ø. Also recommended: A very good large-flowered nostalgic rose is "Paul Noël," repeat-blooming.

My tip: About the fourth year, remove old branches from the inside. Fasten down the young shoots and hold together with a "belly band."

Manou Meilland

Floribunda. Meilland 1977.
Buds medium-sized, elongated, pointed; opens like a hybrid tea. Flowers lilac pink, later dark crimson pink; large, 4 in. (10 cm) Ø; double, some 50 petals; flowers occur in bunches of 3–5; pleasant scent. Very heavy flowering; rainfast. Growth medium-strong, bushy, branching, 23 in. (60 cm) high. Foliage reddish when new, later dark green, large, glossy, leathery, robust. Use as standard especially recommended, crown remains round. Also good as bedding rose for borders and with shrubs.
My tip: Very robust.

Blessings

Hybrid tea. Gregory 1969.
Buds round-oval, large. Flowers delicate salmon pink to coral pink; 3½ in. (9 cm), saucer-shaped, well doubled with 30 petals; 2–4 flowers to a stem but also occurring singly; pleasing fragrance. Heavy bloomer.

Kew Rambler

Manou Meilland

Growth upright, roundly bushy, 31 in. (80 cm) high. Foliage dull green, large. Use as a standard recommended.

My tip: When used as a bedding rose it is prone to spot anthracnose.

Raubritter

Climbing rose/shrub rose. Kordes 1936. *Rosa x macrantha* hybrid.

Blessings

Buds intense pink, round. Flowers light purple pink; small, 2 in. (5 cm) Ø, but well doubled, round until fading, growing alone or in bunches along last-year's canes; delicate fragrance. Very heavy, medium-late flowering but only once. Not rainfast. Growth sturdy, broadly bushy and overhanging, with soft canes, 78 in. (200 cm)

Raubritter

Rosarium Uetersen

Félicité et Perpétué

Chevy Chase

Félicité et Perpétué
Climbing rose (derivative of *Rosa sempervirens*). A. A. Jacques 1827. Buds roundish-pointed, cream-colored, classic. Flowers white, with pinkish cast; small, 1½ in. (4 cm), with 30 petals densely doubled like a rosette; well distributed in clusters and singles; somewhat herbish-sweet scent. Blooms once luxuriantly. No hips. Growth sturdy, elegantly overhanging, over 156 in. (400 cm) high, rambler type. Foliage medium green, small, in some areas not entirely evergreen. Use for arbors and pillars. Very attractive as a cascade rose.
My tip: Tremendous effect from a distance, even the first year. Not entirely rainfast.

Chevy Chase
Climbing rose. N. J. Hansen/ Bobbink & Atkins 1939. Buds small, roundish, dark red. Flowers deep, dark crimson red; small, 1½ in. (4 cm) Ø, very densely doubled like pompoms, 30 petals; in bunches of up to 20; somewhat fragrant. Blooms once but flowers last a long time, are weatherfast, only in extremely hot sun burn along the edges. No hips. Growth stiff at first, canes soon thinner, very vigorous, over 156 in. (400 cm) high, overhanging. Foliage light-green, soft, wrinkled. Use as climbing rose for pillars, walls, arbors. Especially beautiful as a cascade rose. The initially stiff canes form a rather broadly outspread crown.

high, rambler type. Foliage small, coarse, medium green. Use as single planting.
My tip: Very frost-hardy, therefore a first-class cascade rose on a standard. Rain often rots the bud, which should then be cut off. Slightly prone to mildew and red spider.

Rosarium Uetersen
Climbing rose. Kordes 1977. Buds oval in clusters, light red. Flowers pinkish red, later deep rose; large-flowered, 4¾ in. (12 cm) Ø, densely doubled, 30 or more petals, occurring in bunches, slightly fragrant. Very heavy, continuous flowering; rainfast. Growth medium-strong, twiggy-bushy, upright, 78 in. (200 cm) high. Foliage large, medium green, shining, dense, covering well. Use for pillars, low walls, very good on a high standard, then ball-like, not trailing.
My tip: Remove spent flowers to hinder the production of hips too early.

Index

Index

Index / Addresses

Addresses for More Help

Rose Societies

The American Rose Society
PO Box 30,000
Shreveport, LA 71130

The Canadian Rose Society
686 Pharmacy Avenue
Scarsborough, Ont.
Canada M1L 3H8

Heritage Rose Foundation
1512 Gorman Street
Raleigh, NC 27606

The Royal National Rose Society
Chiswell Green
St. Albans, Hertfordshire
England AL2 3N4

Rose Nurseries, Growers, Mail Order Houses

Jackson & Perkins
1 Rose Lane
Medford, OR 97501-0701
1-800-292-4769

Pickering Nurseries
676 Kingston Road / Highway #2
Pickering, Ont.
Canada L1V 1A6
416-839-2111

Roses of Yesterday and Today, Inc.
Watsonville, CA 95076-0398
408-724-2755

Wayside Gardens
1 Garden Lane
Hodges, SC 29695-0001
1-800-845-1124

Rose Gardens & Botanical Gardens

Boerner Botanical Gardens
5879 South 92nd Street
Hales Corners, WI 55130
414-425-1130

Columbus Park of Roses
3923 North High Street
Columbus, OH 43214
614-645-3350

The Cranford Rose Garden
Brooklyn Botanic Garden
1000 Washington Avenue
Brooklyn, NY 11225
718-622-4433

E.F.A. Reinisch Rose Garden
Gage Park
4320 West 10th Street
Topeka, KS 66604
913-272-6150

Elizabeth Park Rose Garden
150 Walbridge Road
Hartford, CT 06119
203-722-6543

Huntington Botanical Gardens
1151 Oxford Road
San Marino, CA 91108
818-405-2100

International Rose Test Garden
400 S.W. Kingston Avenue
Portland, OR 97201
503-248-4302

The Peggy Rockefeller Rose Garden
The New York Botanical Garden
Bronx, NY 10458
212-220-8767

Prospect Park Rose Garden
8205 Apache Avenue NE
Alburquerque, NM 87110
505-296-8210

Reno Municipal Rose Garden
2055 Idlewild Drive
Reno, NV 89505
702-785-2270

Rose Test Garden
1840 Smith Avenue
Thomasville, GA 31792
912-226-5568

Royal Botanical Gardens
P.O. Box 399
Hamilton, Ont.
Canada L8N 3H8

Secrest Arboretum
Ohio State University
1650 Madison Avenue
Wooster, OH 44691
216-263-3761

Tyler Municipal Rose Garden
420 South Rose Park
Tyler, TX 75702
214-531-1200

University of British Columbia
Botanical Gardens
601 N.W. Marine Drive
Vancouver, British Columbia
Canada V6T 1W5

Important Notice

This book explains how to cultivate, prune, and propagate roses in the garden. Wear heavy gloves when handling roses so as not to be injured by rose thorns. Maintain all garden tools so that no one can be hurt by them. Always put them away when you are finished using them. If you receive open wounds while gardening or working with soil, you should visit a doctor in case immunization against tetanus (lockjaw) is needed.

When using pesticides and fertilizers, follow the directions for use exactly. Keep children and house pets away while you are using these substances. Follow the rules for proper handling of pesticides given on page 48. Store pesticides and fertilizers so that children and pets can't get hold of them.

Close every large liquid manure tank with a grate so that children or small animals can't climb or fall in.

Published originally under the title *DER GROSSE GU RATGEBER ROSEN* by Gräfe und Unzer Verlag GmbH, München Copyright © 1993 by Gräfe und Unzer Verlag GmbH, München

English translation Copyright © 1994 by Barron's Educational Series, Inc.

Translated from the German by Elizabeth D. Crawford

All inquiries should be addressed to:
Barron's Educational Series, Inc.
250 Wireless Boulevard
Hauppauge, New York 11788

Library of Congress Catalog Card No. 93-39702

International Standard Book No. 0-8120-1818-4

Library of Congress Cataloging-in-Publication Data

Bünemann, Otto.
  [Rosen. English]
  Roses : the most beautiful roses for large and small gardens : design ideas for rose arbors, trellises, and beds : rose know-how, planting, culture, pruning, overwintering / Otto Bünemann, Jürgen Becker ; color photographs, Jürgen Becker ; drawings, György Jankovics ; [translated from the German by Elizabeth D. Crawford].
    p.   cm.
  Includes index.
  ISBN 0-8120-1818-4 : $13.95
  1. Roses. 2. Rose culture. 3. Roses—Pictorial works. I. Becker, Jürgen. II. Title.
SB411.B9613   1994   93-39702
635.9'33373—dc20   CIP

Printed in Hong Kong
4567 9955 98765432

Photo Credits

The photographs in this book were taken by Jürgen Becker with the exception of: Angermayer/Pfletschinger: pp. 52 top, 53 top, center top; Bünemann: pp. 91 bottom left, 100 left, bottom right, 116 left center bottom, 153 right center bottom, right bottom; Haenchen: p. 138 bottom; Henseler: pp. 50 center top, center bottom, bottom, 51 center bottom, 52 bottom; Himmelhuber: p. 50 top; Hoppe: pp. 5 bottom, 81 bottom, 115; Jensen: pp. 98 left center top, 101, 146 bottom; Kaminski: p. 51 center top; Klose: p. 127 right center top, 136 left bottom, 147 left bottom, 152–153; Kordes: p. 147 right bottom; Nickig: pp. 60–61, 129 left bottom; Reinhard: pp. 88 left center bottom, 91 top left, top right, 96, 129 right center, 138 top, 142–143, 144–145, 146 top, 147 left top, right center; Schäfer: p. 53 center bottom, bottom; Schlüter: p. 51 top; Schwind: p. 52 center top; Silvestris/Bühler: p. 91 right bottom, back flap top center; Silvestris/Jacobi: back flap bottom center; Silvestris/Layer: back cover flap; Silvestris/Riedmiller: p. 88 bottom; Willner: p. 44; Zunke: p. 51 bottom, 52 center bottom.

Acknowledgments

Photographer Jürgen Becker and the publishers are grateful for permission to photograph in the following gardens: Adriaanse, Middelburg, Holland (p. 29); Bennekom, Domburg, Holland (p. 85); Dekker-Fokker, Veere, Holland (p. 65); Dünow, Ratingen, Germany (pp. 68–69); Ghyczy, Swalmen, Holland (pp. 26–27); Greve, Heerlen, Holland (p. 31); Hobhouse, Tintinhull, Yeovil, England (pp. 132–133); Hoffmann, Dortmund, Germany (pp. 11, 150–151); Jonker, Sybekarspel, Holland (pp. 19, 74); Garten Schloss Kalbeck, Weeze, Germany (p. 63); Lippke, Haan, Germany (p. 4, bottom left); Mottisfont, Romsey, England (pp. 104–105); Pfordte, Cappenberg, Germany (pp. 13, 20–21); Roos, Edam, Holland (p. 40); Roosmalen, Rekem, Belgium (p. 73); Stuurmann, Bergen, Holland (pp. 76–77); Verey, Barnsley House, England (pp. 34–35); Garten Kasteel Wijlre, Holland (p. 70); Dt. Rosarium VDR Westfalenpark, Dortmund, Germany (front cover, pp. 2–3, 4 bottom left, 94–95, 124–125); Roseraie d l'Haÿ, Paris, France (pp. 4 top left, 46–47, 62).

Rosa rubiginosa hybrid

Fall Ornaments

When the summer flowers are gone, the wild roses create a fall show with beautiful hips in brilliant colors from orange to red. The juicy flesh of the fruit is a welcome feast for the birds.

Hips of the *Rosa x micrugosa,* globular and densely covered with prickles

Rosa x paulii

Rosa x hibernica

Rosa moyesii "Superba"